I0087630

FOOTBALL MORSELS:

QUARTERBACKS

An Unbiased Analysis of the NFL QB Position

Ranking and Rating the Best of the Modern Era

Julio C Castañeda Jr

DESCRIPTION

The author tackles the subject of comparing quarterbacks from different eras by developing an unbiased methodology to identify the Best Ever. Since changes in the game have affected the statistical significance of performance metrics, the author redefines the QB passer rating into four new comprehensive metrics. First, he corrects the effect of stat inflation. Second, he incorporates the missing dimensions of the quarterbacking position, such as running, scrambling sack avoidance and fumbling. Third, he takes into account the quarterbacks' winning record. Lastly, the final rating metric combines the first three, to assess the total value of the QB performance. With these factors on hand, the author makes an impartial case for the ranking and rating of the top quarterbacks in the modern era of football.

COPYRIGHT

Football Morsels, Sports Morsels. Copyright © 2015 by Julio C Castañeda Jr. All rights reserved. Printed in the United States of America. This book or any portion thereof may not be reproduced or used in any manner whatsoever without the express written permission of the publisher except for the use of brief quotations in a book review or other noncommercial uses permitted by copyright law.

First Edition, Feb 2015
Second Edition, June 2016
ISBN-13: 978-0692371725
ISBN-10: 0692371729
www.sportsmorsels.com

ACKNOWLEDGEMENTS

This book is dedicated to my mom and dad – thank you for always encouraging me to do better. My father often quoted the Cuban poet and revolutionary José Martí, who said: "Every man should plant a tree, have a child and write a book. These all live on after us, ensuring a measure of immortality."

To my boys, Julio Andres, Jorge Luis and Matteo Karolos, we can achieve just about anything if we are willing to put in the work.

Special thanks to those that contributed by tediously proofreading endless versions – Misty, Stephen, KP, Mike and Belinda.

SECOND EDITION

We published the first edition of "Football Morsels: Quarterbacks" in February 2015 after the 2014 NFL season. In this Second Edition, released in June 2016, we updated the QB standings to reflect the incorporation of a more comprehensive data set going back to 1960, as well as the inclusion of the 2015 season. We integrated into our analysis the full set of 1,642 players that have thrown a pass in the AFL/NFL since 1960, as well as enhanced the manner in which we extrapolated the QB sacks and sacked yards pre-1968. This exercise added a couple of inadvertently omitted old-timers to the Best Ever mix and a handful of new QBs that reached the 8-year minimum for qualification. In addition to more data, we also improved the tQBR calculation to take advantage more rigorous statistical tools. While the names stayed the same and the order of the first seven spots remained unchanged, the addition of more data and improved algorithms slightly shuffled the deck on the QB lists – nothing major but mathematically stronger. Finally, we adjusted the scale on the four proprietary QB metrics to align with the original intent of the NFL for the QBPR – an average QB would score 66.7, a good one would score near 90.0 and a poor one near 50.0. A score of 100.0 remains the gold standard for all the metrics.

CONTENTS

PREFACE

Ever since my early teens, I developed a fascination for sports and sports statistics. At that time, I was an avid baseball fan, as I had not yet realized that my playing career would peak in the 6th grade. We did not have much growing up, but I talked my dad into buying the local newspaper so that I could devour the sports pages every day before I headed off to school. My favorite player at the time was Pete Rose, probably because of a book I read in the 7th grade that was very complimentary of his hustle-over-talent approach. I suppose that the talent part resonated with the ever-mounting number of little league strikeouts I was accumulating at the time.

In my chase for knowledge, I would wake up early so I could check the box scores to find out how Charlie Hustle had done the previous night. It was a sad day in our household when the Mean Red Machine was on a West Coast road trip, and the paper did not receive the final scores in time for printing. However, Sundays were especially joyful since The Miami Herald published an extended sports section with a compilation of the Major League standings and statistical category leaders. I would digest the entire page of size-6 font to fill my heart's content – after reading the comics, of course.

Bill James' annual "Baseball Abstract," published in the late seventies and early eighties hooked me for good. His refreshing and innovative "Sabermetric" approach to rate player-value changed the landscape of baseball. A decade later, Oakland's Billy Beane used James' rating methods to build a winning franchise on the cheap, as chronicled in Michael Lewis' book "Moneyball" and subsequent movie.

I soon expanded that same appetite to other games and started following whatever major sports were played at the time – basketball in the winter, baseball in the summer overlapping and football in the fall. I mostly ignored hockey since it was a fringe sport in Miami when I grew up. The Florida Panthers would have to wait another two decades for their inaugural season, and only transplanted New Yorkers and Canadians cared about hockey.

As my obsession with sports statistics grew, I started to keep track of how many regular season games remained and how many my favorite teams would have to win to make the playoffs. How many hits would Wade Boggs have to muster to finally steal a batting title from Tony Gwynn? How many more hits did Pete need to amass yet another 200-hit season? Was Pete's hit streak still alive? I still remember moping for days when his 44-game streak ended. I thought for sure he would catch the great DiMaggio. Years later, with the gambling and game fixing exposed, the Rose balloon would burst into a million pieces. We all make mistakes along the way. I forgive you, Pete. In a karma-filled world, it would be fitting if your penance were that you make the Hall of Fame posthumously. But I digress.

Over time, I began to ask questions that the box scores had not fully answered to my mathematical satisfaction. For example, the "best of all-time" query in any sport is one that is always marred by misjudgments and biases due to allegiances to teams, eras or favorite players. The Mohammad Ali vs. Mike

Tyson (in his prime that is, pre-Buster Douglas, pre-Evander ear biting, pre-face tattooing and pre-threats of child eating) is one that can never be answered. Boxing poses its own problems to the "Greatest of All-Time" question due to its lack of statistically significant overlap. Other than common opponents, none of the other statistics collected, like knockouts, punches thrown or punches landed provide any common ground for standardizing greatness over time because they depend on the quality of the opponent. Ali fought in an era rich with high-caliber challengers like Liston, Frazier, Norton and Foreman. Tyson, on the other hand, plowed through a pile of punching bags. His best challengers were a washed up Larry Holmes and a converted light-heavyweight Evander Holyfield. Reconciling the Ali-Tyson question becomes statistically impossible without common opponents. (It's Ali, by the way).

Conversely, sports like baseball, football and basketball have amassed piles of statistics that overlap and transcend the generation gap. We can analyze the seemingly endless stream of raw sports data to arrive at concrete answers to most of these time-based questions.

In this book, which focuses on ranking and rating football quarterbacks from different generations, the biggest challenge that we need to address is that of statistical inflation. Comparing Bart Starr to Aaron Rodgers is akin to claiming that gas was cheaper in 1960. The national average for a gallon of gas at the beginning of 2015 was less than $2.50. While it may seem like gas is a lot more expensive than in the good old days, in reality, it is about the same when we factor inflation. According to the U.S. Bureau of Labor Statistics, a gallon of gas cost $0.31 in

1960.   When adjusted with their inflation calculator, the equivalent gallon would cost $2.47 today. Therefore, we cannot discount the old timers even if their stats look Lilliputian as compared to the present day video game-like players.

Fortunately, there are statistical methods available to identify, quantify and reconcile these discrepancies. Analytical and regression tools can normalize the data for rule changes and style of play so that we can compare players from different eras objectively.   After normalizing, stats like passing completion percentage, QB passer rating and yards-per-attempted pass become useful for gauging and comparing players who played decades apart.

This book will address some of those questions concerning football quarterbacks. We will present and statistically justify arguments for the best quarterback of the modern era. Moreover, we will introduce several methods for identifying the Best Ever.

Now, how we ask a question is of particular importance as an ambiguous query may result in an incorrect answer.   For example, if we posed the question "who is the best baseball hitter of all-time?" Well, everyone knows that Pete Rose has the most hits, but does that make him the best hitter of all-time? The reality is that Rose was obsessed with breaking Ty Cobb's record and hung around well into his 40s batting near the Mendoza line (a .200 batting average) in order to accumulate enough hits to catch Cobb. When a list of highest career batting average is compiled, Rose is nowhere to be found. However, if posed the question "who collected the most hits in his career?", then the answer would clearly be Pete Rose. A particular Green Bay quarterback comes to mind with this baseball analogy, and we will have plenty of discussion on just where he ranks in the quarterbacking pecking order.

Therefore, it is in how we ask, "Who is the Best of All-Time?" that determines the most correct answer. Data will be presented to answer not only the question of best quarterback ever but also the best pure passer, the best runner and scrambler, the best season, the best normalized season, the best-combined skills and the winningest. Along the way, we will present other statistical observations, anomalies and nuances such as the "Most Overrated QB" or "Career That Could Have Been" as well as short essays on several quarterbacks we found interesting. Some sections are exclusively frivolous; like the one dedicated to the Mannings, and the ludicrous argument that Eli is better than Peyton because he has more rings. We hope you enjoy reading some of this football minutia as much as I enjoyed creating and analyzing it.

However, before we get started, we need to add a few disclaimers. First, I am neither a professional statistician nor a football expert. As an avid sports fan and a Ramblin' Wreck from Georgia Tech mechanical engineer by trade. I have collected over the years enough statistical tools to analyze raw data, to find trends and to make accurate conclusions. My strength has always been in asking too many questions. I am usually not satisfied with standard Wiki answers or the status quo. Unfortunately, in the sports world, there are plenty of "experts" overflowing with bias and ignorance to fill hundreds of senseless programming hours on 24-hr cable sports channels and sports radio. It's amazing how much non-data based opinion gets passed off as "expert" fact, just because some windbag "Sports Reporter" with a microphone in his or her hand reported it.

For this book, it was very helpful that, with the advent of fantasy football leagues, there are abundant resources for raw football data. NFL.com, ESPN.com and pro-football-reference.com were just a few of the sources used for raw data mining. I mention raw data because I specifically stayed away from the proprietary metrics on those sites so that I could form my own opinions and conclusions.

The analytical tools used to contrast and compare data included basic descriptive statistics, curve fitting, regression analysis and analysis of variance (ANOVA). These tools determined valid mathematical conclusions about the data including correlation, trends and statistical significance. When we use the terms "significant" or "outlier" in this book, they refer to their statistical definitions – that two or more sets of data are not the same and that a data point is outside of its normal range. We included the full list of QBs and reference extended charts in the appendices to un-clutter the text.

Finally, I root for my beloved Dolphins because I grew up and lived most of my life in Miami. Dan Marino and Don Shula are South Florida royalty, and I am one of their biggest fans. Accordingly, I absolutely detest the Patriots (because they are so damn good, and the Belichick-Brady tandem reminds me of the Shula-Marino glory days), abhor the annoying J-E-T-S Jets Jets Jets and have a tepid dislike for the bumbling Bills. That said, I have put any home team allegiances and biases aside for this book and focused solely on the data so that I could award greats like Brady, Namath and Kelly a fair chance. As much as I wanted "Dan the Man" to be the best QB ever, the data concluded differently.

THE CHOSEN FEW

To determine the best quarterback of the modern era, we compiled a comprehensive list going back to 1960. We drew a line at 1960 for two reasons. First, since the leagues merged in 1970, the raw data set needed to include the AFL going back to their inaugural season. Second, the quarterback position was not very glamorous or talented before then, statistically speaking of course (apologies to Sid Luckman, Sammy Baugh, Norm Van Brocklin, Y.A. Title and Otto Graham). This is the reason the sixties are usually referred to as the beginning of the modern era of the NFL. If their highlight films were in black and white, then we mostly ignored those quarterbacks. We had a few exceptions to this rule – quarterbacks that overlapped from the fifties into the sixties and met our minimum requirement in the modern era.

From 1960 to 2015, 1,875 players have attempted ~749,000 passes in the NFL, completing ~423,000 for ~5.2 million yards, ~32,000 TDs and ~29,000 interceptions. Just about every position player got into the act, tossing passes on reverses and fake punts and Statue of Liberty plays and every trick play in between. Running backs, wide receivers, tight ends, kickers, punters and even defensive players, lining up on the offensive side, threw the pigskin.

We started the process of determining the Best Ever by narrowing down the field to quarterbacks only, 1,642, and then we placed minimum requirements on seasons, games played and passes attempted. Since QBs used to carry clipboards for a few years before earning the starting role, we decided on eight total seasons with at least five years as the starting QB. To account for injuries and varying number of games played in a season, we placed the minimum bar at 40 total games as starting QB and 5,000 passing yards, which accounted for the equivalent values of starting eight games for five years. This process eliminated the pretenders and by the time we filtered down the field, we had 198 QBs on our list, including 29 active QBs, 19 Hall of Famers, 61 that played in a championship game and a host of others from the less-than-great pile. The Top 20 QB lists presented throughout this book represent roughly the top 1% of all the QBs to play in the modern era – *some very exclusive company*.

The names that did not belong on this Best Ever list became apparent quickly – they often clustered at the bottom of the best-to-worst list. Some of the names near the top were unexpected. However, more surprising still were the household names, and even Hall of Famers, who severely underperformed on the QB metrics. We will have a special section devoted to them.

NEWCOMERS

A crop of new quarterbacks shows promise including Russell Wilson, Andrew Luck, Nick Foles, Robert Griffin III, Kirk Cousins, Ryan Tannehill, Brock Osweiler, Blake Bortles, Derek Carr and Colin Kaepernick. The highly touted freshmen duo of Winston Jamais and Marcus Mariotta enjoyed a typical rookie season full of learning bumps and bruises, but while they will not meet the minimum requirements for a while, it will be entertaining to watch them succeed or fail like many "Can't Miss" QBs before them.

In just four seasons, Wilson has accumulated some very impressive stats, record, and hardware. With a lofty 101.8 QB passer rating and a 46-18 record to date, Wilson led the resurgent Seattle Seahawks to a Lombardi trophy in 2013 and a return trip in 2014. His combination of passing and running skills has been lethal.

Luck's impact in just four seasons is impressive. He is playing with poise and maturity rarely seen in someone his age. His 2015 season, however, proved a tough campaign filled with poor performances, mostly from a nagging shoulder injury. The 2016 campaign will mark a significant marker for him – can he rebound from adversity to continue to progress and lead the Colts to the next level?

Foles, who came into the league the same year as Wilson and Luck, flourished under Chip Kelly's up-tempo no-huddle offense his first couple of years in Philly – his 2013 campaign even ranked in the Top 10 of the Best Ever QBPR. After a winning but statistically rough start in 2014, a mid-season broken collarbone cut short his year. Kelly then shipped Foles off to the Rams in the offseason in a trade for Sam Bradford. Nick struggled mightily in 2015 under Head Coach Jeff Fisher, eventually even losing the starting job. Maybe he can regain his magic in Tinseltown, now that the Rams relocated to LA.

Griffin III took off like a rocket in DC. His rookie season was unparalleled in terms of production, efficiency and excitement. Unfortunately, he has been stuck in reverse every season since and did not even play a down in 2015. He signed a contract with the dysfunctional Cleveland Browns in 2016 so we will see if he recovers the form from his first season. In 2015, Kirk Cousins beat out RGIII straight up for the starting Redskins job, putting up solid numbers, including a 101.6 in QBPR and completing nearly 70% of his passes. Cousins future looks promising as do the resurging Redskins.

Ryan Tannehill has tread water in South Florida since he arrived four years ago. Hopefully, for Dolfans, the new offensive-minded Head Coach, Adam Gase, he can get him to the next level. The Dolphins front office has very high expectations of Ryan, as they mortgaged the house on a $77 million contract extension in 2014.

Brock Osweiler stepped in ably during the 2015 season when Peyton Manning went down with a foot injury. In the offseason, he signed a free-agent contract with the Houston Texans, where he will have to learn a new spread system. He showed some promise with a strong arm and a couple of comeback victories, but the jury is still out on him.

Blake Bortles, besides having a name reminiscent of a wine cooler, drew the short straw when the dumpster fire that has become the Jacksonville Jaguars drafted him. In spite of the losing franchise, he took a step forward in his second year, tossing 35 TDs and improving his QBPR by nearly 20 points to 88.2.

Things are looking up in Oakland in 2016, and most of the good fortune comes from the promising second year of #4, Derek Carr. He pitched a solid season in 2015, throwing 32 TDs and accumulating a 91.1 QBPR. He looks ready to continue to make strides under Head Coach Jack Del Rio.

On the other side of the Bay, the play of Colin Kaepernick has gone backward since the 2012 Super Bowl under then-coach Jim Harbaugh. He has suffered a tumultuous stretch since he lost his starting job in mid-season 2015, with undisclosed surgeries and an unending battle of words with the 49ers front office. New 49ers coach Chip Kelly may stand as his last chance to regain his old form. If any coach can take advantage of Colin's unique passing and running skills, it is Kelly, but he needs to improve his accuracy and decision-making.

As promising as these newcomers looked, we did not consider them for the all-time rankings, because they did not qualify for the minimum number of seasons played. A decade from now, it will be interesting to look back and see which of these QBs fizzle, and which rise to participate in the all-time discussion.

LEVELING THE PLAYING FIELD

To judge the value of quarterbacks impartially over time, first we have to level the playing field. Since the game has changed significantly since the 60s, normalizing the stats of quarterbacks that played in different decades across an evolving game became necessary. Once we achieved that goal, we could then fairly compare the quarterback play in a conservative run offense, like the Bart Starr Green Bay Packers or Bob Griese Miami Dolphins, to those of a pass-happy offense, like the Dan Fouts San Diego Chargers or the Drew Brees New Orleans Saints.

In addition, we need to factor the two games added to the schedule in 1978, which inflated season and career totals. When considering the best career or season of all-time, it would be unfair to rate the quarterbacks by total yardage or TDs since quarterbacks after 1978 enjoyed those two additional games. Furthermore, consider the 2011 season of Aaron Rodgers that by any standards, rated off the charts. His 14-1 Packers had already clinched the number one seed in the playoffs and the prospect of an undefeated season had been lost the week prior. Having nothing to play for, Coach Mike McCarthy sat Rodgers the last game of the season. At the time, with 45 TDs, he was within reach of the coveted "Most TDs in a Season" record of 50 that Brady had set four seasons earlier. Aaron sat out the game fuming as his backup Matt Flynn tossed six TDs in a laugher of a game, ironically setting the Packer single game record for most TDs. This was a stunning feat by Flynn considering the gunslinger that played in Green Bay before Rogers. But to our point, Aaron could have padded his stats and even set the season record for TD's had he played in that meaningless game. So, to be fair, any comparison needed to take into consideration the per-game value of the overall stats.

Another factor that we needed to include was the emergence of the competing AFL in 1960. The nine newly formed AFL teams suddenly diluted the 12-team NFL talent pool to fill rosters spots. There was a clear statistical impact to NFL player stats in the decade of the sixties, and we will discuss this subject at length. Fortunately, the performance normalized when the leagues merged in 1970. Since then, the league has slowly expanded from 26 teams to the current 32 teams and the watering down of the talent pool that occurred in the sixties has not been repeated.

RULE CHANGES

The first area to consider in judging value over time is the rise of passing statistics due to rule changes. Before 1978, defensive backs were allowed to mug, hold, grab and pester receivers anywhere on the field. In 1978, the league implemented the "no contact after five yards" rule, and it drastically affected the game. Also instituted that same year was a change to offensive holding rules that allowed linemen to extend their arms and use their hands in pass blocking. The combination of receivers running unmolested and additional time in the pocket resulted in a passing statistics spike like never before.

Over the next three seasons, a sudden shift in offensive strategy emerged. Teams quickly realized that they could take advantage of the new rules. Consequently, the average number of passes thrown per game suddenly increased from 25 to 32 (see Figure 1). The average number of rushes per game decreased accordingly and by 1980, for the first time, the average team passed the ball as many times as they ran. Not only did they pass more often, but they also completed passes at a higher rate, as the completion percentage increased from 51% to 56% (see Figure 2).

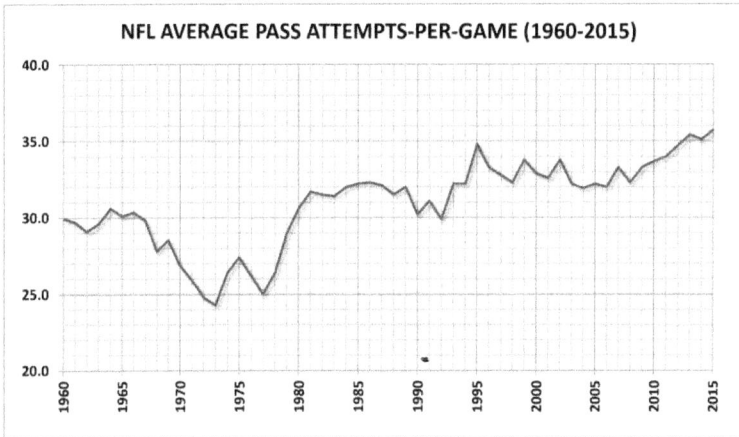

Figure 1 – NFL Pass Attempts per Game

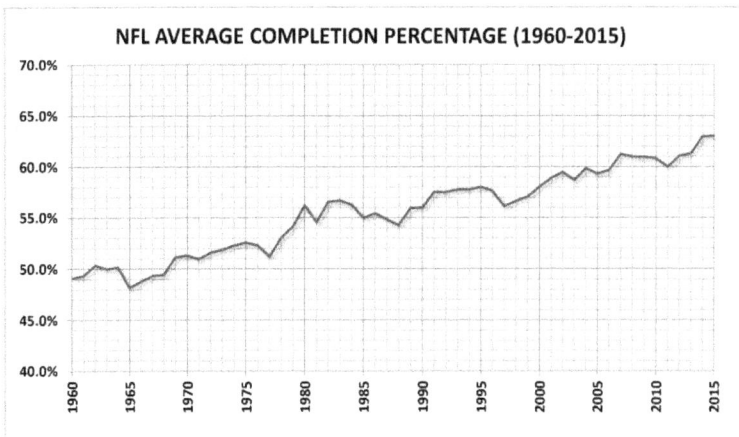

Figure 2 – NFL Average Pass Completion Percentage

Two key performance metrics also increased due to the strategy shift during that period – the touchdown-to-interception ratio and the QB passer rating. The ratio which had been holding steady at 0.8 (four TDs for every five interceptions) for the previous two decades climbed to 1.0 (one TD for every interception) and never looked back (see Figure 3). The QB passer rating also experienced a 14-point spike from 58 to 72 (see Figure 4)! The league was in transition and teams were transformed from mediocre to decent passing offenses virtually overnight.

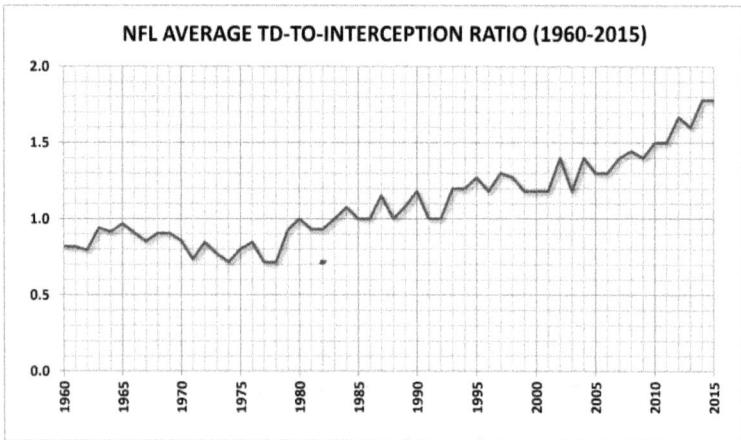

Figure 3 – NFL Average TD-To-Interception Ratio

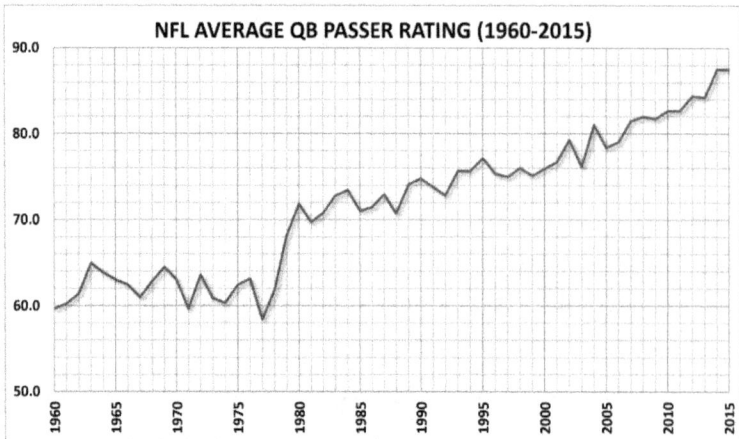

Figure 4 – NFL Average QB Passer Rating

A similar impact due to 1978 rule changes, but on a smaller scale, has taken place in the last decade with the increased enforcement of downfield contact since 2006 and the advent of the "defenseless receiver" rule in 2012. The impact of the latter, especially, points towards another rise in all the significant offensive stats. Time will tell if this trend is part of the normal variation of the data stream, or a significant change that is here to stay like in 1978.

There was also a third related change instituted in 1978 which did not affect the "per game" or "per attempt" stats but wreaked havoc on cumulative records. The season schedule grew from 14 to 16 games. The combination of the rule changes and additional games resulted in a rewrite of all the season and career records for attempts, completions, yards, TDs and interceptions.

OFFENSIVE SCHEME CHANGES

After the no-contact rule, another event in the late seventies contributed to change the passing game forever. By the mid-70s, the number of passes thrown per game had dropped into the mid-20s after a peak in the 60s from the wide-open pass offenses in the AFL (see Figures 5 and 6). The Houston Oilers, the San Diego "Super" Chargers and the Oakland Raiders routinely led the league in passing, throwing the ball more than 30 times-per-game. The passing completion percentage, however, had remained in the low 50s.

The impact of the no-contact rule explained the spike in passes thrown from 1977 to 1980. However, after 1980, the slope of all the key statistical measures (passes attempted per game, completion percentage and TD-to-interception ratio) started to climb steadily. This trend began in the late 70s when a couple of brilliant offensive coaches, named Don Coryell and Bill Walsh, gave birth to new offensive schemes that would, in conjunction with the new rules, revolutionize the offensive side of the ball.

Coryell took over a San Diego Chargers team in 1978 that had, in Dan Fouts, John Jefferson and Charlie Joiner, the building blocks of what his new offensive scheme needed for success. The following year, the Chargers drafted the final piece, TE Kellen Winslow, and the Air Coryell offense was ready for takeoff. Coryell's scheme forced defenses to defend the entire field by stretching the routes of the receivers. He also put players in motion, especially TE and RBs, which caused confusion and assignment mismatches. Winslow was especially cumbersome to defenders – he was too fast for linebackers and too big for cornerbacks. Don's system caught on and about 30% of teams today still use the basis of his offensive strategy.

In 1979, Walsh united with a confident Notre Dame graduate nicknamed "Joe Cool," giving birth to the West Coast offense. The basis of the West Coast offense was simple: a short controlled high-efficiency passing vs. the traditional lower efficiency of the Pro-Style, Smash Mouth or Vertical attacks of that era. The key to the innovative offense was that it provided a low-risk approach to the passing game. Even though the offense attempted more passes, it produced fewer turnovers.

There was one more benefit to their scheme. Before analyzing the data for West Coast vs. traditional passing systems, two markers were expected – higher completion percentage and lower yards-per-attempt. Surprisingly neither materialized. Yes, the completion rates of Montana and his successor, Young, were greater than that of the average quarterback. However, the completion percentage of other elite quarterbacks also increased during that period. When compared to their elite counterparts in the Best Ever list, their passing percentage and QB passer rating were not statistically different.

The second marker was even more unforeseen. *The yards-per-attempt of Montana and Young remained the same as their counterparts in more traditional offenses.* In fact, the league average in yards-per-attempt has virtually not changed since 1960, hovering around 6.3. This was very much unexpected since the basis of the West Coast offense was supposed to be a "controlled low-risk short passing game."

The point is that in a league of copycats, other teams quickly adapted their offenses to incorporate bits and pieces of the Air Coryell and West Coast schemes. Soon everyone was passing more often, completing passes at a higher rate and generally improving their quarterback play. Even today, about 40% of the NFL teams still run a form of the West Coast scheme. The impact of Coryell and Walsh to the passing game is undeniable.

A footnote on a third offense that also grew out of the 70's and is prevalent even today – the Ernhardt-Perkins. This scheme named after a couple of New England coaches, Ron Ernhardt and Ray Perkins, grew under the tutelage of Head Coach Chuck Fairbanks who believed in ball control. This scheme did not progress the passing game like the Air Coryell and the West

Coast offense. The basis of this system was a power running attack with an efficient passing game to complement the ball control attack. About 20% of the teams today use this system, with the Belichick Patriots running the most successful strain.

While Air Coryell never brought any hardware to San Diego, under the West Coast offense, Montana and Young redefined passing efficiency and brought San Francisco five Vince Lombardi trophies in the next two decades. The 60-70's style of three runs and a cloud of dust had met its match. While the no-contact rule switched the offensive attack balance from rushing to passing, the innovative passing game of Coryell and Walsh exploited the defensive weaknesses, and the game changed forever.

CLOCK MANAGEMENT

The previous sections summarized the impact that the rules changes and new offensive schemes had on the game since 1960. From the charts presented, it is clear that all the passing metrics increased significantly over time – this is what economists define as inflation. The following chapter will address the effects of inflation on the individual stats. More importantly, we will present how to undo the inflation so that we can compare quarterbacks from different eras fairly.

Before starting the deflation exercise, let us address three final consequences of rule changes and style of play. First, even though the game has changed drastically from a run to a pass-oriented offensive attack, the average number of offensive plays per team per game has remained unchanged at around 60 plays (Figure 6).

The league realized that more passing meant more incompletions and time stoppages. To combat this trend, which was pushing the length of a televised game past the 4-hour mark, the league came up with a very effective strategy. To keep the game moving and make it more palatable for TV viewers, they changed the rules to maintain the clock running. Under the old rules, the clock would stop after incomplete passes or running out of bounds, then restarted when the ball was snapped on the next play. Under the new regulations, the clock stopped temporarily until a 25-second play clock was started. The NFL has continued to tweak the clock management rules over the years, and they have been incredibly effective in maintaining the number of total plays per team at 60.

Second, a spike in run plays occurred (gray bars) in the mid-seventies followed by a rise in pass plays (black bars) starting in 1978 with the advent of the no-contact rule (Figures 5 and 6). After 1980, the league turned pass-happy, and there has only been one season, 1983, that teams ran more than passed.

Lastly, the number of runs has continued to decrease from a peak of 37 in 1977 to a low of 26 in 2015. Passing, on the other hand, increased in equal and opposite proportion from a low of 24 in 1977 to a high of 36 in 2015.

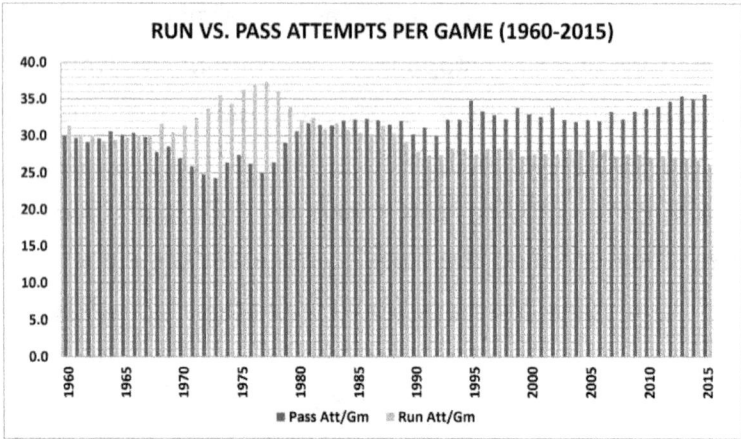

Figure 5 – NFL Total Run/Pass Attempts per Game

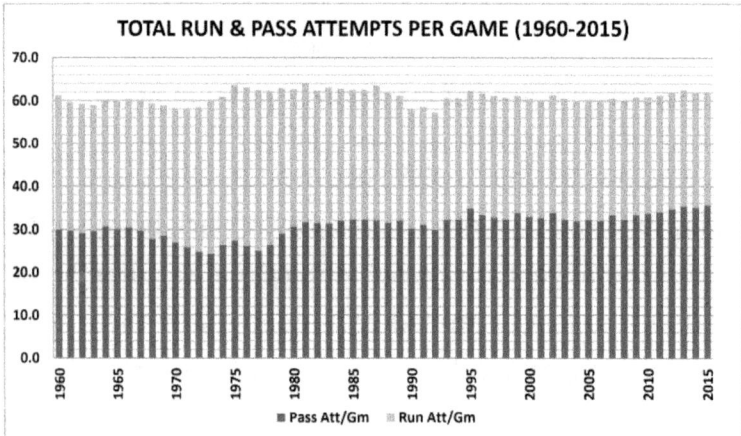

Figure 6 – NFL Run vs. Pass Attempts per Game

NFL QB PASSER RATING

To measure the quality of a quarterback, we need to start by examining how the NFL derived the cryptic QB passer rating (QBPR). The current NFL passer rating uses a weighted system with four components:

- Completion percentage
- Yards-per-attempt
- TDs-per-attempt
- Interceptions-per-attempt

The rating assigns a value between 0 and 2.375 for each of those four parameters. Their sum is then divided by six and multiplied by 100 to return the final rating. Since each of the four parameters is capped at a maximum value of 2.375, the highest QB passer rating possible is 158.3. To achieve a perfect score, a quarterback needs to attempt a minimum of 10 passes, complete at least 77.5%, average more than 12.5 yards-per-attempt, toss TDs on 11.9% or more of those attempts and throw no interceptions.

From 1931-1972, before the current system was instituted, the NFL used several methods to crown a passing leader:

- 1932-1937: by total passing yards
- 1938-1940: by completion percentage
- 1941-1972: various forms of an inverse ranking system based on total completions, yards, TD passes, completions, interceptions and average gain per attempt.

Finally, after the NFL hired a committee in 1971, consisting of football and statistical experts to develop this metric, the current rating system was adopted in 1973. The committee analyzed NFL passing data from 1960 to 1970 to develop this odd formula. Why did they use a value of 2.375 and divide by six then multiply by 100? The answer is simple – they manipulated the formula to standardize performance for the data they collected. An ordinary passer would score 66.7, an outstanding QB near 90.0 and a poor one around 50.0. During the sixties, the league "average passer rating" fluctuated between 60 and 70. There were only eight season ratings over 95, and only three over 100. The committee did their job – they developed a perfectly balanced formula for the NFL decade of the 60's! Well almost – there is a catch.

MISSING DATA

We need to present one more piece of information, which explains the "drop off" in QB passer rating during the early and mid 70's until the rule change of 1978. When the committee chose the raw data to generate the QB passer rating formula, *they ignored the AFL stats, using only the passing data from the NFL.* The AFL played from 1960-1969 and forced the merger in 1970 when the Jets and Chiefs won back-to-back Super Bowls III and IV. Why the committee would not use the AFL data in 1971 when the AFL-NFL merger had already occurred the year before is baffling. This point is critical to mention because the "league average" level of quarterback play in the AFL was significantly lower than in the NFL during the sixties.

Whether the oversight happened on purpose or not, statistically speaking, this was a huge mistake on the part of the committee. The committee calibrated the metric for the NFL "average passer" to score 66.7 (actually 66.4 according to the historical data). However, the league "average passer" in the AFL for that same decade scored 58.8. When the leagues combined, the average passer in 1970 dropped overnight about four points to 62.6.

Description	NFL	AFL	Combined
1960-1969 QBPR	*66.4*	*58.8*	*62.6*

The next chart (Figure 7) clearly shows the discrepancy in the data from 1960-1970:

- Dark gray line: NFL average rating
- Light gray line: AFL average rating
- Dashed line: combined AFL-NFL average rating

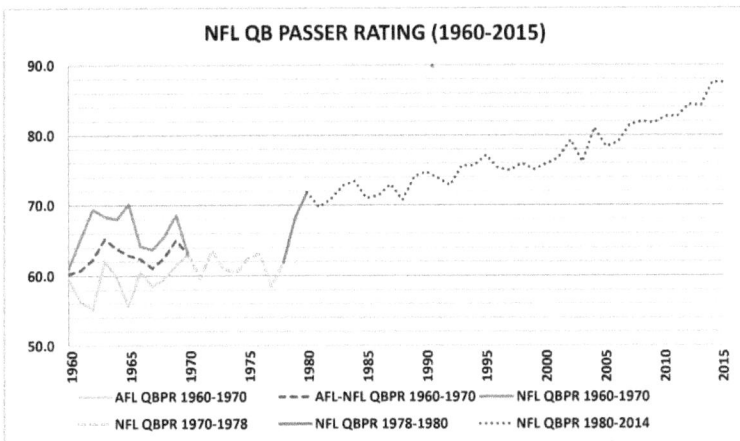

Figure 7 – NFL QB Passer Rating plus AFL

This discrepancy may not seem like much, but for addressing the rate of inflation over time, this hiccup wreaks havoc with the data and regression algorithms. For the purpose of this book, we included both the AFL and NFL stats from the sixties. It is more representative of the post-merger football world and eliminated the data discrepancies before 1970 caused by the committee's oversight.

HIGH PERFORMERS

Since the committee used a benchmark of 100 QBPR for excellence, the table below shows the number of elite quarterbacks that eclipsed the 100 mark per decade since 1960 using the standard NFL QBPR formula. For this exercise, the quarterback had to start a minimum ten games per season.

Decade	NFL QBPR >100
1960-1969	4
1970-1979	3
1980-1989	4
1990-1999	21
2000-2009	46
2010-present (2015)	44

According to this table, the passer rating metric was still hanging on to its validity until the eighties when all hell broke loose. Since 1990, the number of quarterbacks breaking 100 has exploded. The last five years alone has already produced as many "great passers" than the entire previous decade. Undoubtedly, this was not what the committee intended.

The definitive proof stands in the All-Time Top 20 quarterback ranking (Figure 8) using the standard NFL QBPR formula, which yields some very questionable results. Rodgers heads the list, which is not too crazy, as he has accumulated some very impressive numbers in his 11 years. After that, the list breaks down quickly. Romo, Rivers, Pennington, Schaub, Palmer, Culpepper, Garcia and Green make the Top 20 scattered with the likes of Young, Peyton, Brady, Montana, Staubach, Marino and Favre. This just does not pass the common sense test.

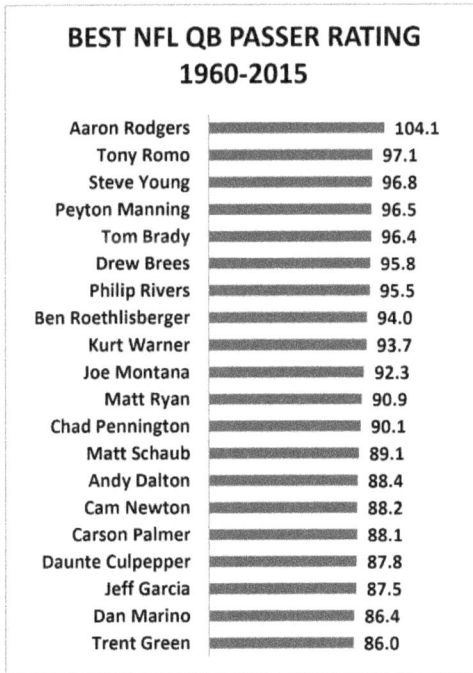

BEST NFL QB PASSER RATING
1960-2015

Aaron Rodgers	104.1
Tony Romo	97.1
Steve Young	96.8
Peyton Manning	96.5
Tom Brady	96.4
Drew Brees	95.8
Philip Rivers	95.5
Ben Roethlisberger	94.0
Kurt Warner	93.7
Joe Montana	92.3
Matt Ryan	90.9
Chad Pennington	90.1
Matt Schaub	89.1
Andy Dalton	88.4
Cam Newton	88.2
Carson Palmer	88.1
Daunte Culpepper	87.8
Jeff Garcia	87.5
Dan Marino	86.4
Trent Green	86.0

Figure 8 – Top 20 NFL QB Passer Rating Since 1960

Looking at the QBPR formula now, it makes little sense why the NFL is still using a metric with outdated correlation data and no inherent compensation for stat inflation. The committee in 1971 had no inkling of the coming rule changes or style of play that would render their compilation of odd multipliers non-factors within the first decade of implementation. By 1980, the formula needed some adjustments. A decade later, it had been rendered obsolete.

The reason that the formula became obsolete is not that it is a bad recipe. The inputs are correct. Passing efficiency should be measured using the core parameters of the passing game: attempts, completions, yards, TDs and interceptions. The problem is that the committee chose poorly for the raw data pool by ignoring the AFL stats, so right out of the gate, the metric was off by almost 4 points. Since the metric was based on fixed data from the sixties, there was no way to handle the rise in scores due to rule changes or stat inflation. The ranking chart makes the point very clear that the metric needs adjustment.

Okay, then to fix the metric, we adjust the weight of the four components, tweak the multiplier and we're done, right? Not really. Besides the factors that are obsolete, there is another huge drawback to the QB passer rating metric – *it is only a measure of pure passing*. The formula does not account for other crucial quarterback metrics like sacks, sack yards, rushing attempts, rushing yards, rushing touchdowns or fumbles. From the standpoint of the NFL QB passer rating, a rushing phenom like Michael Vick gets no credit for his Houdini-like running ability to escape pressure vs. a pocket stiff like Bernie Kosar. Therefore, to develop a more accurate formula not only does it need to address the obsolescence of the QB passer rating method, but it also needs to encompass all the dimensions of the quarterback position including sack avoidance and run related metrics.

INFLATION-ADJUSTED QBPR

We will tackle the flaws in the QB passing rating metric in two ways. First, we will adjust the passer rating for inflation. Second, we will include the missing parameters related to rushing, scrambling, sack avoidance and fumbling.

INFLATION ADJUSTMENT

We will use a powerful statistical tool called regression analysis to adjust the NFL passer rating and eliminate the effect of statistical inflation over time. Rather than updating the old scores to the ballooned ratings of today, we will maintain the original intent of the committee. An average QB will score 66.7, a good passer will record a score near 90.0 and a poor one around 50.0. Like before, an outstanding performance will rate around 100.0. Therefore, we will deflate the recent scores back to the 60's and, in essence, we will pay less than a $1 for gas again!

The method is straightforward. Analyze the four metrics to develop the best-fit regression curve then plug all the new values back into the original formula to adjust all the ratings back to their 60s level. Using this method eliminates the need to re-invent the original formula. It is a good recipe – it just needs a little love and a chiropractic adjustment.

COMPLETION PERCENTAGE

The number of passes completed per attempt has steadily increased since 1960 from 49% completion to 62%, a jump of 13% (Figure 9). The regression curve has an R-Squared value of 94%. This probably does not mean much to the average fan, but in statistics, the R-Squared determines the correlation of the data to the regression model, with a score between 0 and 100%. In this case, a linear model explains 94% of the variation in the data, which makes it an excellent predictor. We will skip these tedious statistical details going forward in the text, but for reference, we will include the R-Squared in the charts.

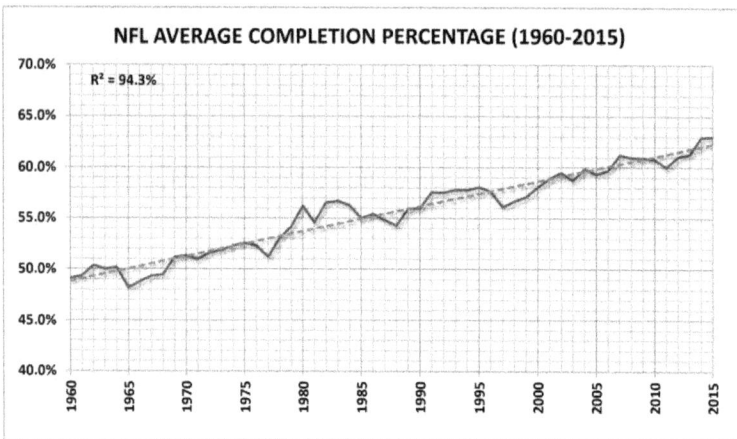

Figure 9 – NFL Average Completion Percentage Trend

YARDS-PER-ATTEMPT

Even though the total passing yards have increased from 175 to 235 per game, the yards-per-attempt has remained surprisingly steady over the course of five decades. Defenses are holding well against the pass over the last 55 years as shown by the lack of change in the "yards-per-attempt" chart (Figure 10). The only blip on the chart is a dip in the 70s then the correcting spike for the no-contact rule change in 1978. Since then it has remained virtually flat.

Note that the yards-per-game have increased because teams attempted more passes, not because the yards-per-pass improved. We established this earlier – that teams pass about ten more times a game today than they did in the 70s.

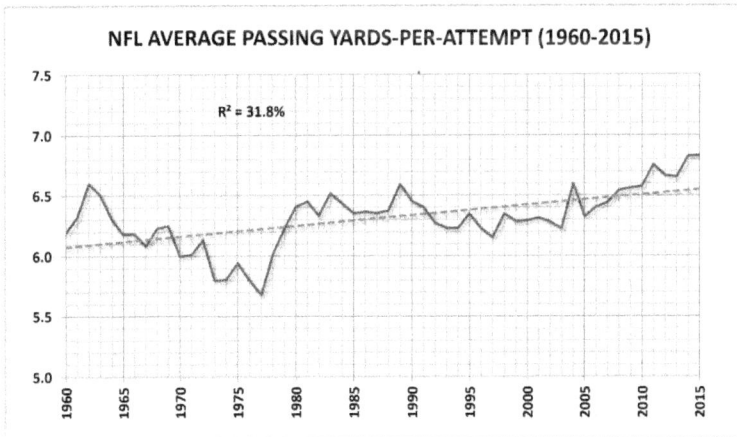

Figure 10 – NFL Passing Yards-per-Attempt Trend

TDS-PER-ATTEMPT

The number of passing touchdowns has increased dramatically but not as a percentage of the passes thrown (Figure 11). In fact, the percent of touchdowns-per-attempt decreased from a peak of 5.5% in 1960. The ratio bottomed out at 4.0% at the turn of the century and started to climb steadily to 4.5% in the last 15 years.

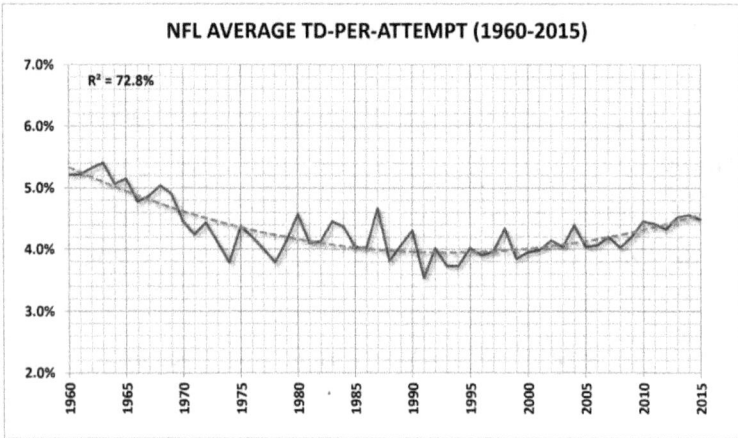

Figure 11 – NFL Average TD-per-Attempt Trend

INTERCEPTIONS-PER-ATTEMPT

The total number and percentage of interceptions dropped like a rock from a peak of more than 6% in 1960 to around 2.5% in 2015. We touched on this subject briefly when discussing the touchdown-to-interception trends reversing. Whoever is pulling the strings on this miracle at NFL headquarters should immediately go to the White House and apply the same principles to the unemployment rate.

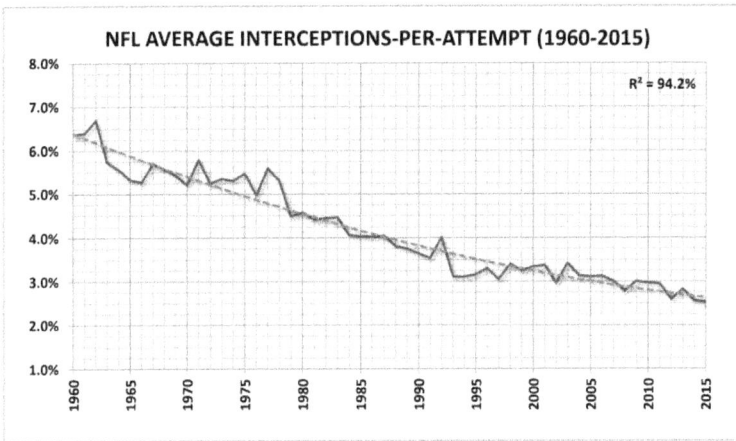

Figure 12 – NFL Average Interception-per-attempt Trend

TOUCHDOWNS-TO-INTERCEPTIONS

The critical ratio of touchdowns-to-interceptions, because it quantifies goodness-to-badness, has more than doubled from 0.8% to over 1.7%. In 1960, quarterbacks tossed fewer touchdowns than interceptions at a clip of four to five. Today, an average quarterback throws more than three touchdowns for every two interceptions. This massive reversal continues to widen due to the enforcement of the "no downfield contact" and the newly implemented "defenseless receiver" rules.

To put those numbers in perspective, in 2015, the average QB tossed 26 TDs to 14 interceptions – numbers that QBs in the 60s and 70s would only dream about achieving. Oh, and by the way, today, those totals get the average NFL starting QB a contract for about $17 million-a-year.

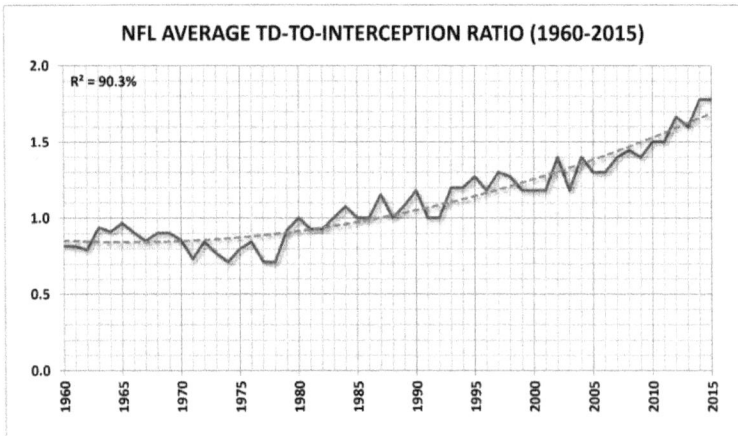

Figure 13 – NFL Average TD-To-Interception Ratio Trend

ADJUSTED QB PASSER RATING (aQBPR)

As the chart shows below (Figure 14), a single regressions curve adjustment does not fully address the unexpected QBPR changes that have occurred since 1960. When we consider the entire data set, the best-fit regression curve falls short of the AFL-induced peaks in the sixties, ignores the sudden spike in 1978 then does a fair job of aligning the data from 1980 to today.

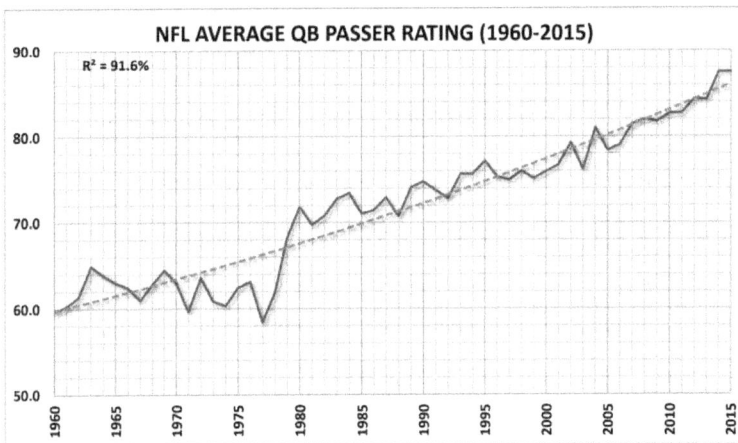

Figure 14 – NFL Average QB Passer Rating Trend

However, we can do better. If instead of clumping the entire data set together, we break up the response into three segments, then we can achieve a highly correlated response. The split consists of:

- A flat response from 1960 to 1970 to align to the AFL-NFL cumulative data set
- An extended flat response from 1970 to 1978
- A linear rise from 1978 to 1980 to account for the rule changes of 1978
- A fitted polynomial regression curve from 1980 to 2015

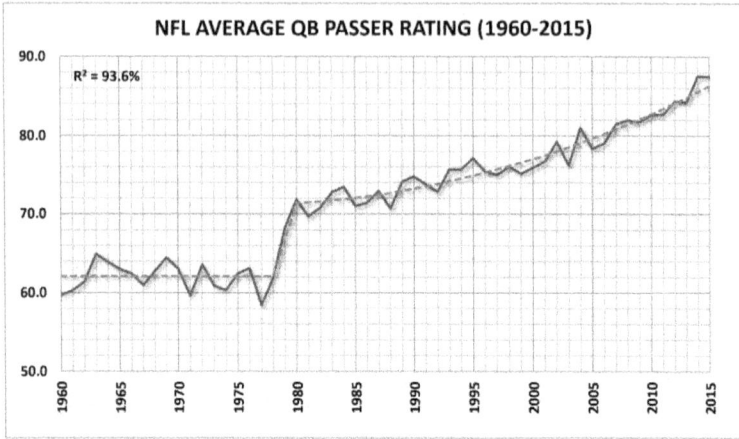

Figure 15 – NFL QBPR and Inflation Adjustment Factor

With this new response on hand, we can reverse the inflation factor of the QB passer rating over the years very accurately. So let's put the adjustment formula to work and see what happens to elite performances since 1960. Using the NFL metric, there have been 242 total scores greater than or equal to 90, 136 ≥ 95 and 67 ≥ 100. When the "inflation adjusted" passer rating formula is applied, a much more palatable distribution forms for elite performances.

	>100		>95		>90	
	QBPR	Adjusted QBPR	QBPR	Adjusted QBPR	QBPR	Adjusted QBPR
1960's	4	4	10	10	19	19
1970's	3	3	4	4	13	12
1980's	4	2	13	4	34	11
1990's	12	1	21	5	41	17
2000's	21	2	48	3	77	13
2010's	23	2	40	4	58	9
TOTAL	67	14	136	30	242	81

Figure 16 – NFL QB Passer Rating Vs. Inflation-Adjusted QBPR

The previous chart (Figure 16) showed the effect of re-rating those 242 scores. The inflated total number of scores drops significantly to 81 (>90), 30 (>95) and 14 (>100), respectively. Additionally, the number of "inflation adjusted" scores is consistent ranging from 11 to 19 from decade to decade, thereby achieving the initial desired result – reward an outstanding performer with a score of 100.

MODIFIED QB RATING (mQBR)

Now, we will take on the tougher part of the passer rating discrepancy. We need to address the exclusion of the non-passing dimensions of the quarterback position. An updated total quarterback rating metric would need to account for other quarterback stats like sacks, sack yards lost, rushing attempts, rushing yards, rushing TDs and fumbles lost. In addition, we need to apply the deflation factor to this formula. When we added the missing metrics to the pure passing stats and compensated for inflation, we achieved a more comprehensive picture of the overall value of the quarterback position.

A note about sacks – the NFL does not count sacks against the quarterback's passing stats, only against the team stats. Also, when the quarterback gets sacked, even though it is a failed pass attempt, the NFL does not count it as a pass attempt. Furthermore, the league does not count the yards lost on a sack against the quarterback's passing yards; they count them against the team's passing yards. The logic is that we should not punish the quarterback for one of his linemen allowing a pass rusher to get by him or a receiver's inability to shake a defensive back. The counter argument is that when the quarterback holds on to the ball too long, his protection will eventually breakdown yielding a sack. Sacks also lead to another important statistic – fumbles lost. The majority of QB turnovers come as the result of getting banged around in the pocket (unless protected by the infamous "Tuck Rule" but let's not go there). We will include the sack and sack yard parameters in the modified passer rating metric.

Lastly, at some point in their careers, some quarterbacks have caught a few passes, and even touchdown passes as part of trick plays. Even though these totals rate as mostly inconsequential, we added receiving yards and touchdowns to their totals, just to be thorough.

To define the new modified QB rating metric, mQBR, we expanded the four main weighted categories of the QBPR to include the additional parameters of rushing, sacks, receiving and fumbles:

1. Completions-per-attempt: the pass attempts will include sacks and run attempts.

2. Yards-per-attempt: the passing yards will include rushing yards, receiving yards and sack yards lost. The pass attempts will include sacks and run attempts.

3. TDs-per-attempt: the passing TDs will include rushing TDs and receiving TDs. The pass attempts include sacks and run attempts.

4. Interceptions (turnovers)-per-attempt: the interceptions will include fumbles lost. The pass attempts include sacks and run attempts.

We first applied the modification to the QBPR without an inflation adjustment to assess the impact of the combined quarterbacking skills (Figure 17). Since the passing game is more efficient than running/sacks in terms of yards per play, all the QBPR ratings dropped accordingly. The interesting part is that the mQBR of great runners like Vick, Culpepper, Staubach and Young lost more points than the pure passers who were sacked less.

The new metric, mQBR, was highly correlated to three factors: passing yards-per-attempt, sacks-per-attempt and running yards-per-attempt. However, the significance of each of those factors was not equal. Passing influences the mQBR more than twice as sacks, which in turn, affects it more than twice as rushing. *The result of the modified formula is that taking fewer sacks is more important than running for positive yards but passing trumps both of those factors.*

Figure 18 shows the running game regression analysis on the difference between the QBPR and the mQBR. The results is somewhat surprising -- higher rushing yards (achieved on a per-game or a per-attempt basis) has bigger negative impact on the mQBR. For example, Vick runs for 43 yards-per-game and 7.0 yards-per-attempt, but his mQBR dropped 23.5 points, as compared to his QBPR.

Accordingly, two of the least sacked QBs, Peyton and Marino, moved up the mQBR list even though they are among the worst runners ever. Alternatively, running sensations Culpepper, Vick and Cunningham and dropped significantly because of their inability to avoid sacks, rating at 41st, 44th and 51st, respectively.

Note that the charts below (Figure 17 and 18) do not account for inflation or winning aspects, and we will address those in the next chapters.

MODIFIED QB PASSER RATING
mQBR* (1964-2015)

Quarterback	mQBR
Peyton Manning	86.5
Aaron Rodgers	84.6
Drew Brees	83.7
Tom Brady	81.6
Tony Romo	81.3
Philip Rivers	79.1
Joe Montana	78.2
Matt Ryan	78.0
Steve Young	76.3
Ben Roethlisberger	76.1
Dan Marino	75.3
Matt Schaub	75.1
Carson Palmer	75.0
Andy Dalton	74.7
Kurt Warner	74.4
Chad Pennington	73.5
Matthew Stafford	73.3
Jeff Garcia	72.2
Brett Favre	71.3
Trent Green	70.0

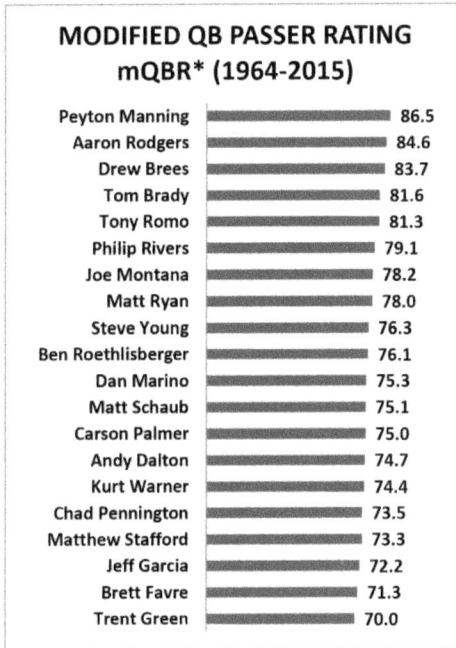

Figure 17 – Top 20 Modified QB Passer Rating, mQBR (* No Inflation)

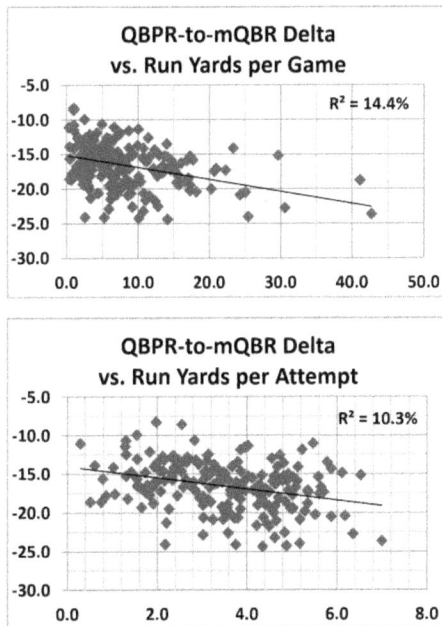

QBPR-to-mQBR Delta
vs. Run Yards per Game

$R^2 = 14.4\%$

QBPR-to-mQBR Delta
vs. Run Yards per Attempt

$R^2 = 10.3\%$

Figure 18 – Regression Analysis of QBPR-to-mQBR vs. Running Ability

BEST PERFORMERS BY CATEGORY

As indicated in the Preface, the question of the greatest QB needs to be scrutinized thoroughly. Since how the question is asked is just as important as the answer, the discussion will be broken down into several categories, and then a data-based case will be presented for the Best Ever.

THE BEST PURE PASSER

We used the four metrics that compose the QBPR to compare and contrast the best passing quarterbacks: completion percentage, yards-per-attempt, TDs-per-attempt and interceptions-per-attempt. We then used the inflation-adjusted QB passer rating, aQBPR, to crown the Top 20 Best Pure Passers.

COMPLETION PERCENTAGE

When we eliminate the effects of inflation on the completion-per-attempts statistics (Figure 19), Montana and Young sit atop the best completion percentage list moving up from 13th and ninth, respectively. Their West Coast offensive system really pays off on this list.

Pennington makes a surprise showing on both lists ranking second and third. His reputation for owning a weak but accurate arm landed him near the top, where precision and efficiency pays off. Pretenders Schaub, Palmer, Cutler and Green drop out of the Top 20 when we adjust and thereby expose their inflated numbers. Warner came in fifth, dropping only one place, maintained by his legendary accuracy.

COMPLETION PERCENTAGE (1960-2015)

Player	Percentage
Drew Brees	66.4%
Chad Pennington	66.0%
Kurt Warner	65.5%
Peyton Manning	65.3%
Tony Romo	65.3%
Aaron Rodgers	65.1%
Philip Rivers	64.8%
Matt Ryan	64.3%
Steve Young	64.3%
Ben Roethlisberger	64.1%
Matt Schaub	64.0%
Tom Brady	63.6%
Joe Montana	63.2%
Daunte Culpepper	63.0%
Carson Palmer	62.7%
Brian Griese	62.7%
Andy Dalton	62.3%
Marc Bulger	62.1%
Jay Cutler	62.0%
Shaun Hill	62.0%

ADJUSTED COMPLETION PERCENTAGE (1960-2015)

Player	Percentage
Joe Montana	57.7%
Steve Young	57.3%
Chad Pennington	56.6%
Bart Starr	56.6%
Kurt Warner	56.2%
Drew Brees	56.1%
Ken Stabler	56.1%
Sonny Jurgensen	55.8%
Peyton Manning	55.6%
Ken Anderson	55.6%
Len Dawson	55.5%
Billy Wade	55.3%
Fran Tarkenton	54.9%
Danny White	54.8%
Tony Romo	54.7%
Dan Fouts	54.5%
Aaron Rodgers	54.3%
Philip Rivers	54.2%
Troy Aikman	54.2%
Bob Berry	54.2%

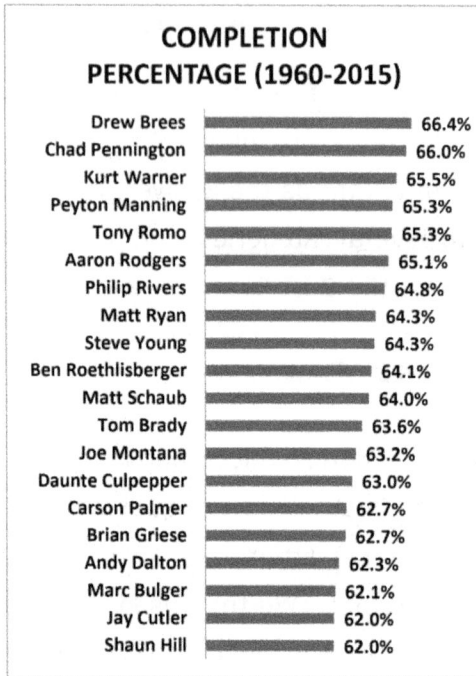

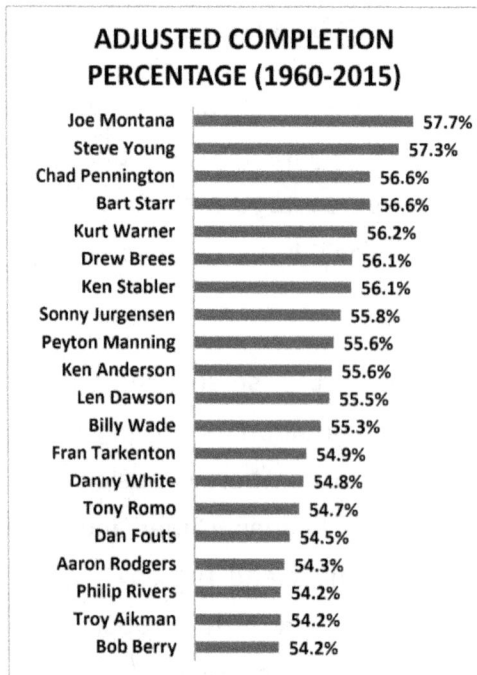

Figure 19 –Top 20 Completion Percentage and Adjusted

Since the average completion percentage ballooned by 13% from 1960 to 2015, some QBs from the sixties and seventies shined on the adjusted chart. Starr jumped up from 74th to fourth while Jurgensen and Dawson also make the Top 20. Stabler also makes a big jump, moving up from 38th to seventh.

The top two names from the inflated list, Brees and Rodgers, drop several spots to sixth and 17th. Peyton dropped from fifth to ninth while Roethlisberger and Brady dropped from tenth and twelfth to out of the Top 20 altogether.

YARDS-PER-ATTEMPT

In this category, since the yards-per-attempt have stayed mostly consistent over the years, the names on the two lists remaining roughly the same but are shuffled slightly (Figure 20).

Rodgers drops from first to tenth. Young moves up from second to first. Warner drops from third to eighth. Big Ben drops from fourth to 12th.

Berry, Starr, Morrall, Unitas and Dawson represent the sixties well, moving up several spots into the adjusted Top 10. Fouts makes an appearance as his Air Coryell offense lifted him from #11 to seventh. Likewise, Staubach moves up from 13th to sixth.

More recent players in Peyton, Green, Schaub, Culpepper, Newton and Brees dropped out of the adjusted Top 20.

PASSING YARDS-PER-ATTEMPT (1960-2015)

Player	Value
Aaron Rodgers	8.01
Steve Young	7.98
Kurt Warner	7.95
Ben Roethlisberger	7.93
Tony Romo	7.89
Bart Starr	7.85
Bob Berry	7.84
Earl Morrall	7.79
Philip Rivers	7.76
Johnny Unitas	7.76
Dan Fouts	7.68
Len Dawson	7.67
Roger Staubach	7.67
Peyton Manning	7.67
Trent Green	7.61
Matt Schaub	7.60
Sonny Jurgensen	7.56
Daunte Culpepper	7.55
Cam Newton	7.55
Drew Brees	7.53

ADJUSTED PASSING YARDS-PER-ATTEMPT (1960-2015)

Player	Value
Steve Young	7.96
Bob Berry	7.92
Bart Starr	7.89
Earl Morrall	7.84
Johnny Unitas	7.79
Roger Staubach	7.76
Dan Fouts	7.76
Kurt Warner	7.74
Len Dawson	7.74
Aaron Rodgers	7.64
Sonny Jurgensen	7.61
Ben Roethlisberger	7.60
Joe Montana	7.57
Frank Ryan	7.56
Steve Grogan	7.56
Tony Romo	7.55
Lynn Dickey	7.54
Billy Wade	7.54
Craig Morton	7.52
Bill Nelsen	7.50

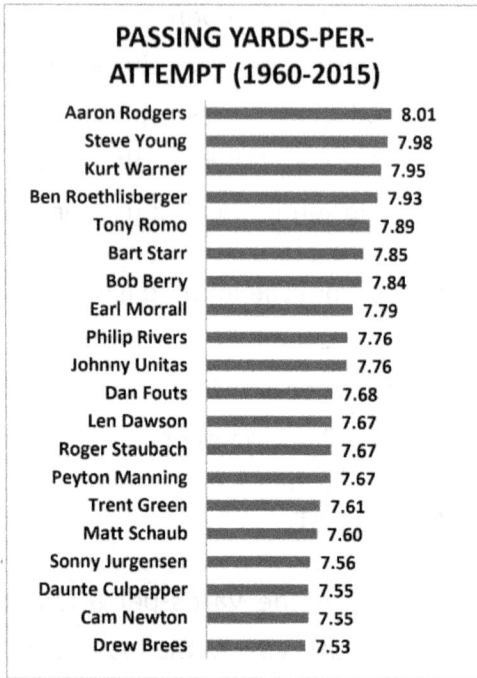

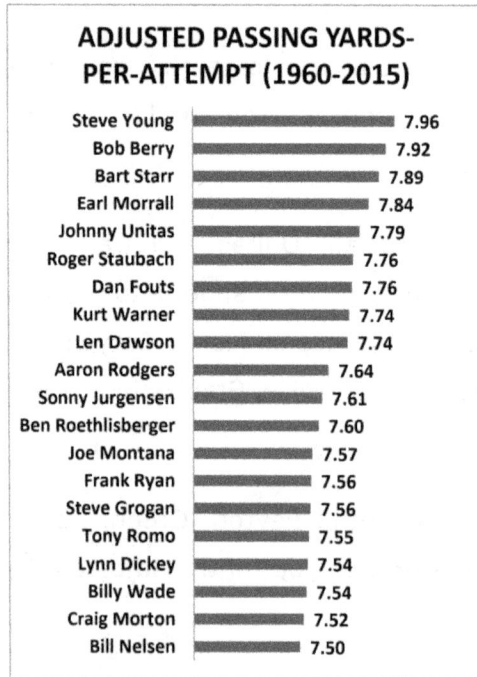

Figure 20 –Top 20 Passing Yards-Per-Attempt and Adjusted

TDS-PER-ATTEMPT

In the touchdowns-per-attempt category, Frank Ryan leads both lists (Figure 21). An interesting side note on the last Browns QB to lead Cleveland to a championship – Frank stands as the only QB to play in the NFL after receiving a Ph.D. degree (Mathematics from Rice University).

Rodgers rated third and second on the lists but note that since the TD-per-attempt percentage has actually decreased over time, Rodgers has an adjusted percentage that is higher than the non-adjusted value. Young placed third on the adjusted list, while the fourth name on both lists, Daryle Lamonica, did not surprise. The vertical attack of the Oakland Raiders favored the long ball and The Mad Bomber became infamous for long TD passes. Dawson performed well on the adjusted list, coming in fifth.

Griese is a name that jumps out of the page, in particular that he ranks ahead of the other Dolphin great, Marino, on both lists. It is unforeseen what happens when these categories when viewed on a per-attempt basis instead of just a career total!

Romo surprised with ranks of 10th and seventh, and especially that he placed ahead of Brady on both lists. The other name that surprises is Favre. When we normalize his 500+ career TDs on a per-attempt basis, he does not even crack the Top 20 on the standard list and ranks 20th on the adjusted version. This is due to the Rose Accumulation Theory that we will cover in the Bonus Morsels section.

PASSING TD-PER-ATTEMPT (1960-2015)

Frank Ryan	6.99%
Len Dawson	6.39%
Aaron Rodgers	6.35%
Daryle Lamonica	6.31%
Sonny Jurgensen	5.98%
Earl Morrall	5.97%
George Blanda	5.89%
Don Meredith	5.85%
Peyton Manning	5.75%
Tony Romo	5.70%
Bob Griese	5.60%
Johnny Unitas	5.59%
Steve Young	5.59%
Tom Brady	5.49%
Bob Berry	5.46%
Terry Bradshaw	5.43%
Babe Parilli	5.39%
Tom Flores	5.38%
John Hadl	5.38%
Drew Brees	5.29%

ADJUSTED PASSING TD-PER-ATTEMPT (1960-2015)

Frank Ryan	7.30%
Aaron Rodgers	7.29%
Steve Young	6.96%
Daryle Lamonica	6.94%
Len Dawson	6.94%
Peyton Manning	6.87%
Tony Romo	6.68%
Tom Brady	6.54%
Danny White	6.50%
Bob Griese	6.47%
Terry Bradshaw	6.47%
Sonny Jurgensen	6.44%
Dan Marino	6.38%
Joe Montana	6.38%
Earl Morrall	6.37%
Jim Kelly	6.33%
Drew Brees	6.32%
Kurt Warner	6.31%
Dave Krieg	6.26%
Brett Favre	6.26%

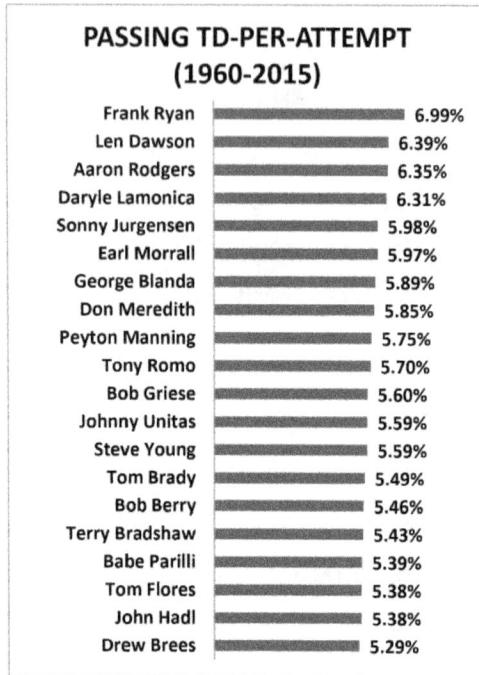

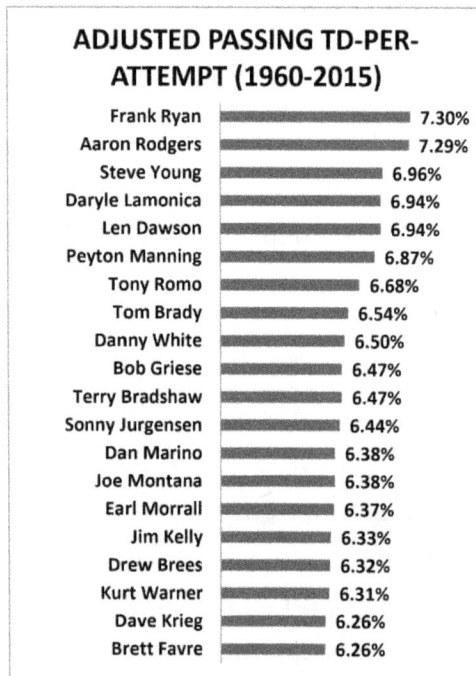

Figure 21 –Top 20 Passing TD-per-Attempt and Adjusted

INTERCEPTIONS-PER-ATTEMPT

The interception-per-attempt has dropped incredibly over the years, from over 6% in 1960 down to 2.5% in 2015 – a more than two times reduction. The effect of the rule changes and downfield policing has dramatically changed this metric over the years. The best example of this effect is Rodgers, who in 11 years in the league has tossed only 65 interceptions. To catch Favre's 336-career total accumulated over 20 years, Rodgers would have to play for 57 years!

On the current inflated list, Rodgers and Brady, at #1 and #2, ring in below 2% (Figure 22). Because of the massive deflation, however, journeymen from the last two decade fill the Top 20 list: O'Donnell, McNabb, Garcia, Bradford, A. Smith, Brunell, M. Ryan, Campbell, Garrard, Orton, Graham, Bono, Gannon and Hill. The last three names on the list (Rivers, Brees and Montana) finally make some sense. Expectedly, no one from the sixties or seventies even sniffs a spot on the Top 20.

When the inflation calculator reverses the rise in the metric, we turn the list upside down. Unexpectedly, 49ers QB Roman Gabriel leads adjusted list followed by a nice spread of QB's from all the decades. In the old-timers category from the 60s and 70s, along with Gabriel, Starr came in second and was also joined on the list by Carter, Munson, Jurgensen, Tarkenton, Staubach, Dawson, Meredith and Unitas.

From the 80s and 90s, Montana placed third along with Lomax, Kosar, O'Brian, Bono, Young and Eason. From the last 15 years, O'Donnell leads at fifth followed by Rodgers and Brady.

INTERCEPTIONS-PER-ATTEMPT (1960-2015)

Aaron Rodgers	1.61%
Tom Brady	1.93%
Neil O'Donnell	2.11%
Donovan McNabb	2.18%
Jeff Garcia	2.26%
Sam Bradford	2.27%
Alex Smith	2.29%
Mark Brunell	2.33%
Matt Ryan	2.36%
David Garrard	2.37%
Jason Campbell	2.38%
Kyle Orton	2.44%
Kent Graham	2.46%
Steve Bono	2.47%
Rich Gannon	2.47%
Joe Flacco	2.51%
Shaun Hill	2.52%
Philip Rivers	2.53%
Drew Brees	2.54%
Joe Montana	2.58%

ADJUSTED INTERCEPTIONS-PER-ATTEMPTS (1960-2015)

Roman Gabriel	4.25%
Bart Starr	4.79%
Joe Montana	4.91%
Virgil Carter	4.97%
Neil O'Donnell	5.00%
Bill Munson	5.00%
Sonny Jurgensen	5.06%
Neil Lomax	5.09%
Fran Tarkenton	5.10%
Bernie Kosar	5.15%
Ken O'Brien	5.17%
Roger Staubach	5.18%
Aaron Rodgers	5.25%
Ken Anderson	5.26%
Don Meredith	5.29%
Johnny Unitas	5.30%
Steve Bono	5.31%
Steve Young	5.35%
Tony Eason	5.42%
Tom Brady	5.45%

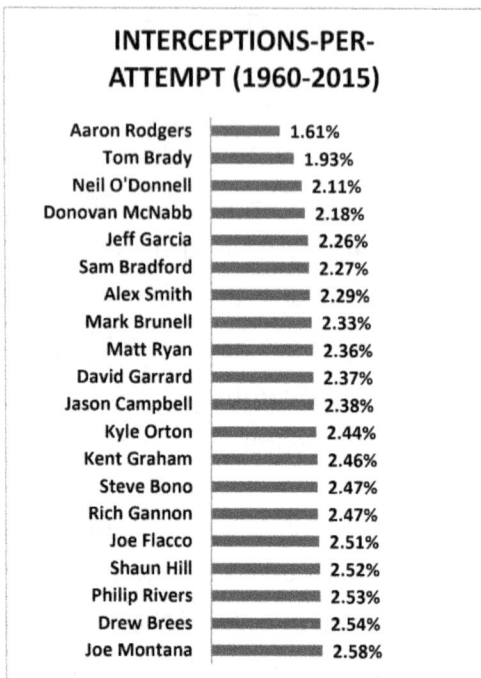

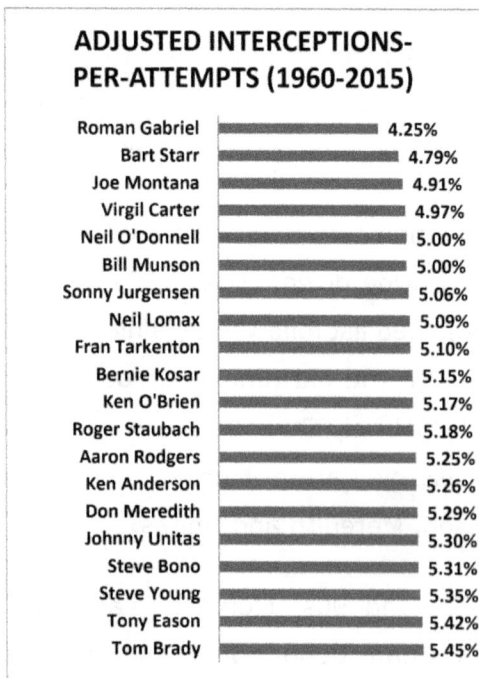

Figure 22 –Top 20 Interception-per-Attempt and Adjusted

ADJUSTED QB PASSER RATING (aQBPR)

We compared the original NFL QB passer rating, QBPR, to the inflation-adjusted aQBPR to crown the leaders in this category (Figure 23). Rodgers sits atop of the QBPR list as the only quarterback with a career rating in triple digits at 104.1. His scores rates seven points above second place Romo at 97.1 (no, that is not a typo) who squeaks past Young and Peyton at 96.8 and 96.5, respectively. Brady, Brees, Rivers, Roethlisberger, Warner and Montana fill the rest of the Top 10. It is no surprise that there are no names from the sixties or seventies on this stat-inflated list.

It is a much different story on the inflation-adjusted aQBPR chart. Aaron comes back to Earth when we adjust his rating, and his large margin from the QBPR list disappears. He led this list at the end of the 2014 season, but with a subpar 2015 campaign, Rodgers dropped to second on the list behind *Young, who claims the title of Best Pure Passer*. The rest of the Top 10 on this list in order includes Montana, Dawson, Jurgensen, Staubach, Starr, Tarkenton, Peyton and Brady.

All the decades earn decent representation on the adjusted list:

- 1960-1969: Dawson, Jurgensen, Starr, Unitas and Ryan
- 1970-1979: Staubach, Tarkenton, Anderson, Berry, and Griese
- 1980-1999: Montana, Marino
- 1991-1999: Young, Warner
- 2000-2015: Rodgers, Peyton, Brady, Romo, Brees and Philips

QB PASSER RATING
QBPR (1960-2015)

QB	Rating
Aaron Rodgers	104.1
Tony Romo	97.1
Steve Young	96.8
Peyton Manning	96.5
Tom Brady	96.4
Drew Brees	95.8
Philip Rivers	95.5
Ben Roethlisberger	94.0
Kurt Warner	93.7
Joe Montana	92.3
Matt Ryan	90.9
Chad Pennington	90.1
Matt Schaub	89.1
Andy Dalton	88.4
Cam Newton	88.2
Carson Palmer	88.1
Daunte Culpepper	87.8
Jeff Garcia	87.5
Dan Marino	86.4
Trent Green	86.0

ADJUSTED QB PASSER RATING
aQBPR (1960-2015)

QB	Rating
Steve Young	86.5
Aaron Rodgers	84.7
Joe Montana	84.0
Len Dawson	82.9
Sonny Jurgensen	82.7
Roger Staubach	82.4
Bart Starr	80.4
Fran Tarkenton	80.1
Peyton Manning	80.1
Tom Brady	78.8
Kurt Warner	78.6
Ken Anderson	78.5
Tony Romo	78.2
Johnny Unitas	78.2
Frank Ryan	77.9
Drew Brees	77.9
Bob Berry	77.7
Dan Marino	76.9
Philip Rivers	76.4
Bob Griese	76.3

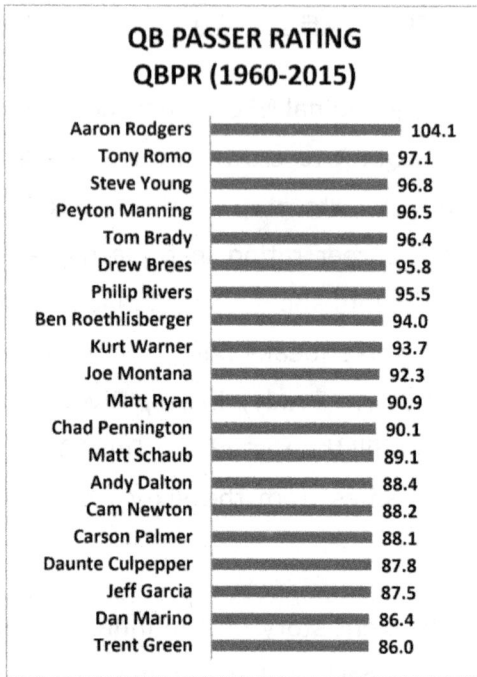

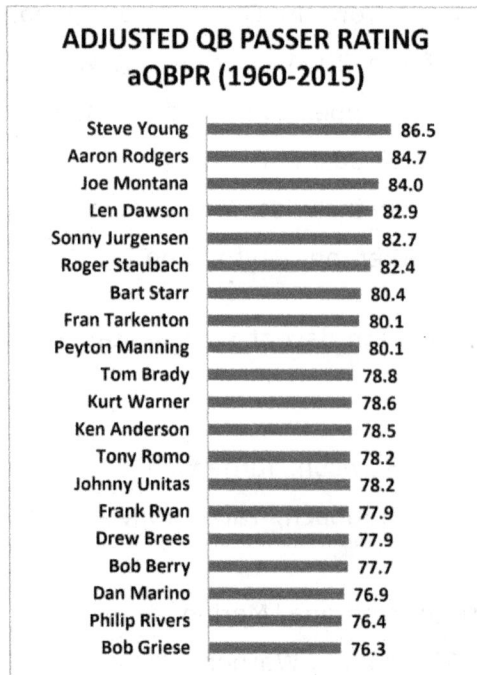

Figure 23 –Top 20 QBPR and aQBPR (Adjusted)

THE BEST RUNNER/SCRAMBLER

The capability of a quarterback to scramble and create plays on the run has long been revered. Only a few of the QBs on the list can boast the ability to extend plays while their counterparts would have gone down in a heap. In the seventies, Fran "The Mad Scrambler" Tarkenton and Roger "The Dodger" Staubach were renowned for their scrambling ability. In the eighties and nineties, Elway and Young gained reputations as great runners and scramblers. In the last 25 years, numerous QBs with outstanding running ability have sprouted in the NFL.

With the advent of the Modern Era, other than a quarterback sneak for a first down or a kneel-down at the end of a half, QBs rarely executed any rushing plays by design. Occasionally, they would run the goal line trick play where the QB would fake a hand-off, keep the ball and hustle into the end zone on a naked reverse. Yet, more often than not, runs typically resulted out of desperation by the quarterback in order to escape the rush when the defense successfully blanketed the receivers downfield.

That would all change, however, when a tall, lanky kid made the Philadelphia Eagles squad in 1985 and redefined the running aspect of the quarterback position. Over the next 16 years, Randall Cunningham would accumulate over 4,900 rushing yards, adding a dimension to the position that did not exist prior to his arrival. He was such a great runner that the Eagles soon started to design running plays specifically to take advantage of his rushing skills. Others teams began to draft QBs with the added dimension of mobility and soon a handful of "running" QBs sprouted around the league.

We must note, however, that the capacity to run needs to complement the ability to pass, not become the primary weapon. With their lack of passing skill exposed, a number of these running QB draftees turned into huge busts. Names like Kordell Steward, Akili Smith, Andre Ware and, more recently, Vince Young and Tim Tebow come to mind.

It is no surprise that Michael Vick sits atop both QB rushing lists, amassing more than 6,000 career rushing yards and 43.6 rushing yards-per-game (Figure 24). His predecessor and first successful running QB, Cunningham, comes in second and third on these lists.

Cam Newton ranks second on the per-game list, a shade below Vick. They rank as the only two players with rushing averages over 40.0 yards-per-game. Currently eighth, he will undoubtedly continue to rise on the career yards list, as he just seems to have hit his stride in 2015.

Longtime reputed runners and scramblers litter both the career and per-game lists: Young, Tarkenton, Douglass, Culpepper, McNair, Stewart, Staubach, McNabb, Elway and Grogan.

While Fran "The Mad Scrambler" and Roger "The Dodger" received most of the acclaim from the 70's as the best scramblers, their nemesis, Bradshaw, also ran very well and racked up a very respectable 2,257 rushing yards in his career. Also, another name that surprised on the per-game list, Rodgers, snuck in at 17th, with an understated running ability even though he continues to take too many sacks. Which leads to the next topic.

QB RUSHING CAREER YARDS (1960-2015)

QB	Yards
Michael Vick	6,109
Randall Cunningham	4,928
Steve Young	4,239
Fran Tarkenton	3,727
Steve McNair	3,590
Donovan McNabb	3,459
John Elway	3,407
Cam Newton	3,207
Tobin Rote	3,128
Kordell Stewart	2,851
Jim Harbaugh	2,787
Greg Landry	2,655
Daunte Culpepper	2,646
Bobby Douglass	2,578
Rich Gannon	2,449
Mark Brunell	2,421
Roger Staubach	2,264
Terry Bradshaw	2,257
Ken Anderson	2,220
Steve Grogan	2,176

QB RUSHING YARDS-PER-GAME (1960-2015)

QB	Yards per Game
Michael Vick	42.7
Cam Newton	41.1
Randall Cunningham	30.6
Bobby Douglass	29.6
Daunte Culpepper	25.4
Steve Young	25.1
Vince Young	24.3
Kordell Stewart	23.4
Steve McNair	22.3
Tobin Rote	21.0
Donovan McNabb	20.7
David Garrard	20.3
Greg Landry	18.2
Doug Flutie	17.7
Roger Staubach	17.3
Jeff Garcia	17.3
Aaron Rodgers	17.3
Jeff Blake	17.0
Ryan Fitzpatrick	16.8
Aaron Brooks	16.5

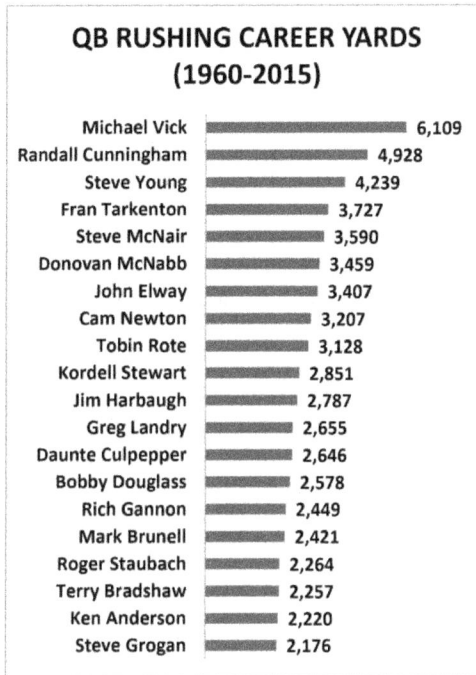

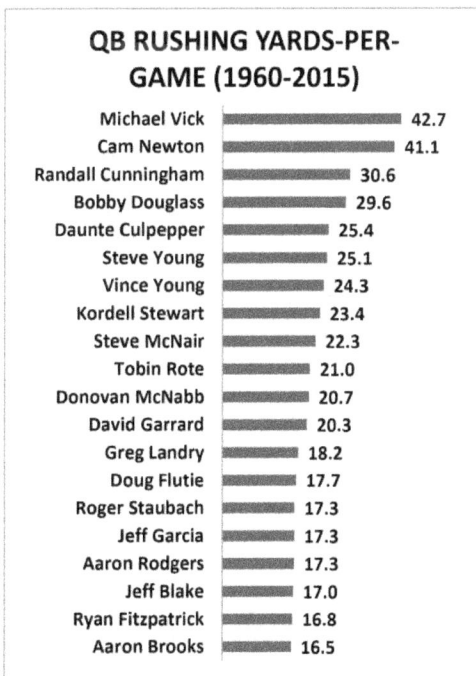

Figure 24 –Top 20 QB Career Rushing Yards & Yards per Game

THE LEAST SACKED

On the least sacked QB list, *Peyton and Marino separated themselves from the rest of the field tied for first at 3.13% sacks-per-attempts.* Even though they both had the running ability of the Statue of Liberty, they also had a reputation for a quick release and the innate ability to slide in the pocket to avoid the oncoming pressure.

Not known for his flashy running or scrambling, Williams ranked a strong third place while Blanda, Rypien and Brees scored the only other percentages under 4.0%. Other notable QBs including Namath, Eli (as Patriot fans can attest), Brady and Favre placed in the Top 10 least sacked QBs.

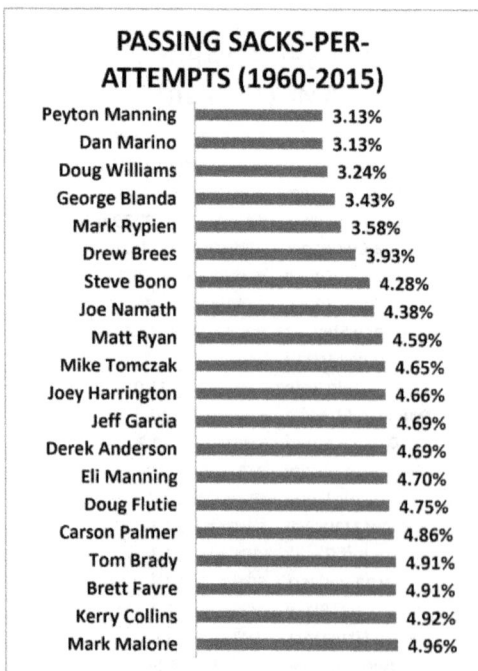

PASSING SACKS-PER-ATTEMPTS (1960-2015)

QB	%
Peyton Manning	3.13%
Dan Marino	3.13%
Doug Williams	3.24%
George Blanda	3.43%
Mark Rypien	3.58%
Drew Brees	3.93%
Steve Bono	4.28%
Joe Namath	4.38%
Matt Ryan	4.59%
Mike Tomczak	4.65%
Joey Harrington	4.66%
Jeff Garcia	4.69%
Derek Anderson	4.69%
Eli Manning	4.70%
Doug Flutie	4.75%
Carson Palmer	4.86%
Tom Brady	4.91%
Brett Favre	4.91%
Kerry Collins	4.92%
Mark Malone	4.96%

Figure 25 –Top 20 QB Run-Sack Yards/Game & Sacks/ Attempt

THE BEST SEASON

There have been many great QB seasons over the years – Marino's 1984 Beamonesque attack on the record books, Warner's 1999 dream season, Peyton's 2004/2013 mammoth years, Rodgers' and Brees' 2011 monster seasons and Brady's epic 2007 campaign. If we only ranked the seasons only by cumulative yards and TDs, then Peyton's 2013 campaign with 5,477 yards and 55 TDs runs away with just about every category. However, we need to frame any discussion about the Best Season with statistical outliers relative to previous performances, and, more importantly, calibrated for inflation. *It is no coincidence that the majority of these great seasons were recorded in the last decade*.

To choose the best QB season ever, we judged the leaders by the principal categories of completion percentage, yards, TDs and interceptions. Since the QB passer rating combines these four metrics, we used the QBPR and inflation adjusted aQBPR to crown a winner. We only considered seasons that the QB met a minimum number of passes and games played. Since the schedule changed in 1978 from 14 to 16 games, the minimum threshold based on the year are 275 attempts before 1978 and 300 after. The QB needed to play in a minimum of half of the games, seven before 1978 and eight after. To eliminate bias for the number of games played, we focused on normalized metrics (either per-game or per-attempt). Finally, we will reverse the factor of inflation, which affected the results tremendously.

When we ranked the data by the standard QBPR, Rodgers won outright with his 2011 season score of 122.5 (Figure 26).

In the Top 10 of the QBPR list, only two QBs logged seasons before 2000, Young in 1994 and Montana in 1989. Warner's 1999 and Marino's 1984, record-breaking campaigns at the time, ranked a measly 16th and 17th.

When we applied the inflation adjustments, however, a different story emerged. Of the seasons that qualified for the minimum requirements, 73 had scores that broke the 100.0 barrier with the standard QBPR. After we had adjusted for inflation, only 13 remained using the aQBPR.

Without inflation, little known Milt Plum takes the top spot with a phenomenal 110.4 rating in 1960 no less. His rating was so outrageously out of proportion for his time that we dedicated a chapter in the Bonus Morsels section just for him.

Of the more conventional names on the list, Peyton's 2004 at 106.2 would have rated as the best season ever. Starr's 1966 score of 105.0, jumped from 23rd to third. Staubach's 1976 tied with Y.A. Tittle's 1963 for fourth, both scoring 104.8 ratings. Unfortunately for Tittle, he did not play enough seasons in the Modern Era to qualify on our list of All-Time QBs.

Montana's 1989 season ranked sixth (103.7). Stabler's 1976 season (103.4) soared from 31st on the QBPR list to seventh. Rodgers' 2011 (103.3) and Young's 1994 (102.5) came next at eighth and ninth. The last four spots in the 13 seasons with scores over 100 were taken by Jones' 1976 (102.5), Dawson's 1966 (101.7), Marino's 1984 (101.3) and Brady's 2007 season (100.6).

BEST PASSING SEASON QBPR (1960-2015)

Player	Season-Score
Aaron Rodgers	2011-122.5
Peyton Manning	2004-121.1
Nick Foles	2013-119.2
Tom Brady	2007-117.2
Peyton Manning	2013-115.1
Tony Romo	2014-113.2
Steve Young	1994-112.8
Joe Montana	1989-112.4
Aaron Rodgers	2014-112.2
Tom Brady	2010-111.0
Daunte Culpepper	2004-110.9
Drew Brees	2011-110.6
Milt Plum	1960-110.4
Russell Wilson	2015-110.1
Drew Brees	2009-109.6
Kurt Warner	1999-109.2
Dan Marino	1984-108.9
Aaron Rodgers	2012-108.0
Brett Favre	2009-107.2
Steve Young	1992-107.0

BEST ADJUSTED PASSING SEASON aQBPR (1960-2015)

Player	Season-Score
Milt Plum	1960-110.4
Peyton Manning	2004-106.2
Bart Starr	1966-105.0
Roger Staubach	1971-104.8
Y.A. Tittle	1963-104.8
Joe Montana	1989-103.7
Ken Stabler	1976-103.4
Aaron Rodgers	2011-103.3
Steve Young	1994-102.5
Bert Jones	1976-102.5
Len Dawson	1966-101.7
Dan Marino	1984-101.3
Tom Brady	2007-100.6
Len Dawson	1968-98.6
Nick Foles	2013-98.6
Len Dawson	1962-98.3
Steve Young	1992-97.4
Johnny Unitas	1965-97.4
Bart Starr	1964-97.1
Kurt Warner	1999-96.9

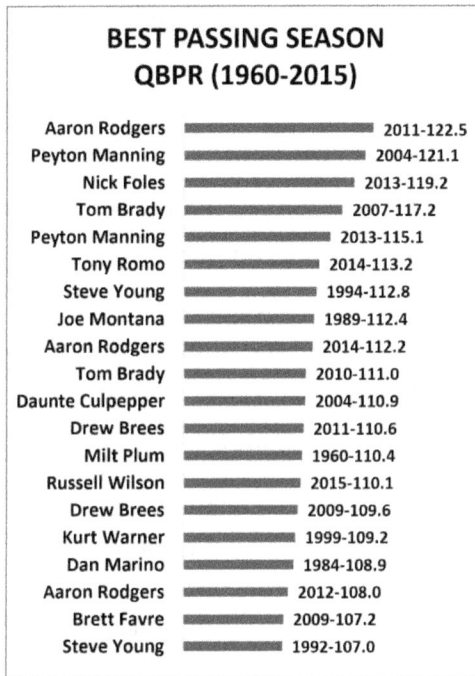

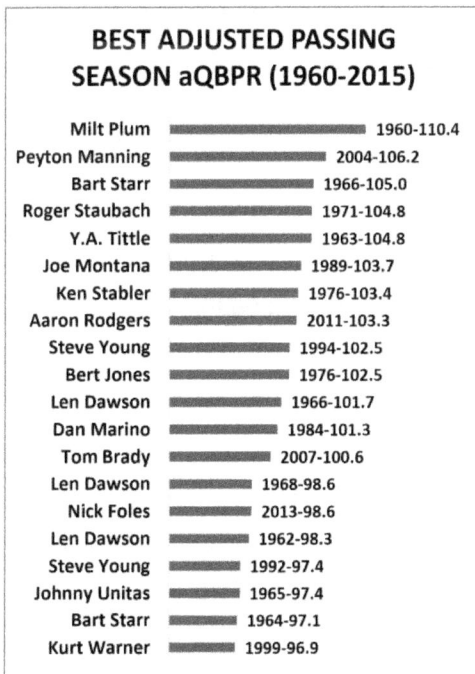

Figure 26 –Top 20 Season QBPR and aQBPR (Adjusted)

THE BEST NORMALIZED SEASON

We have another more efficient manner to measure the best season, instead of the best stand-alone individual metrics from the previous section. We can normalize the season numbers to eliminate the influence of missing games (due to injury), shorter seasons or number of pass attempts (due to the style of play) that affect the per-season total. Since the yards-per-attempt has not changed much over time, the number of attempted passes per game has a tremendous impact on the total yards per game or season. For example, comparing QBs from different eras in average attempts showed a huge discrepancy:

- Brees, Warner and Peyton averaged 596, 566 and 566 attempts, respectively
- Starr, Griese and Dawson averaged 321, 363 and 376 attempts, respectively

Accordingly, their total yards per game and season ring up almost twice as that of their counterparts from the sixties and seventies who played with offensive styles that severely limited their passing opportunities. To compensate for this discrepancy, we presented the normalized season numbers for passing yards and TDs in three distinct ways. First, we took the accumulated career totals divided by the number of games started, then multiplied by 16 to output the equivalent of one full season. Second, we used the same calculation but adjusted for inflation. Lastly, we took the same calculation as #2 but adjusted for inflation and normalized to 31 attempts per game to give the players from the sixties and seventies a fair chance. We used 31 since that is the average attempts per game from 1960 to 2015.

NORMALIZED – AVERAGE GAME X16

Accumulated career totals divided by the number of games started multiplied by 16 to output the equivalent of one full season

The normalized passing yards-per-season charts placed Brees, Stafford, Warner, Rodgers, Peyton, Schaub, Romo, Brady, M. Ryan and Rivers in the Top 10 (Figure 27).

In the TDs-per-season, Blanda, Rodgers, Peyton, Brees, Romo, Brady, Lamonica, Warner, Rivers and Stafford placed in the Top 10.

As expected in both of these "not adjusted for inflation" lists, recent and current active players fill most of the spots with a few old-timer names sprinkled about the Top 20. On the yards list, only three of the QBs played before 1990 – Marino, Montana and Blanda. In Blanda's case, his inclusion came from his years with the high-powered offense of the AFL Houston Oilers.

In the TD list, a few more old timers worked their way into the Top 20 – Blanda, Lamonica, Parilli, Jurgensen, F. Ryan and Meredith.

NORMALIZED PASS YARDS-PER-SEASON (1960-2015)

Player	Yards
Drew Brees	4,511
Matthew Stafford	4,469
Kurt Warner	4,461
Aaron Rodgers	4,356
Peyton Manning	4,344
Matt Schaub	4,322
Tony Romo	4,303
Tom Brady	4,163
Matt Ryan	4,160
Philip Rivers	4,145
Dan Marino	4,091
Gary Hogeboom	4,080
Ben Roethlisberger	4,071
George Blanda	4,063
Trent Green	4,032
Carson Palmer	4,029
Dan Fouts	4,027
Wade Wilson	4,008
Steve Bono	3,977
Joe Montana	3,956

NORMALIZED PASS TD-PER-SEASON (1960-2015)

Player	TD
George Blanda	35.6
Aaron Rodgers	34.6
Peyton Manning	32.5
Drew Brees	31.7
Tony Romo	31.1
Tom Brady	30.7
Daryle Lamonica	29.8
Kurt Warner	28.7
Philip Rivers	28.1
Matthew Stafford	28.0
Dan Marino	28.0
Babe Parilli	28.0
Sonny Jurgensen	27.8
Frank Ryan	27.4
Brett Favre	27.3
Joe Montana	26.6
Carson Palmer	26.1
Danny White	26.0
Don Meredith	26.0
Steve Young	26.0

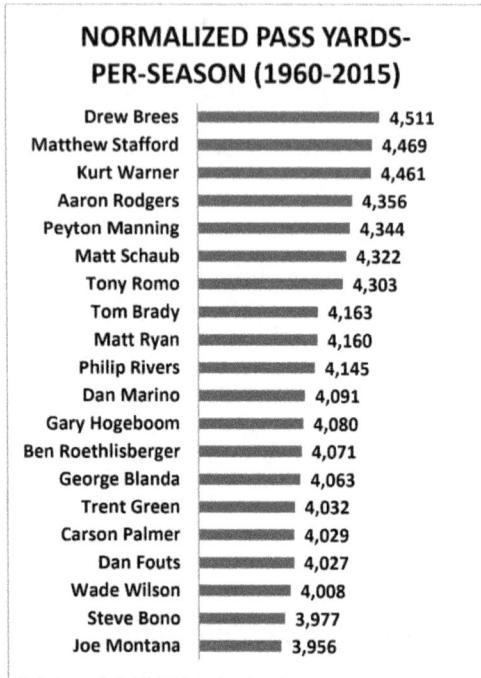

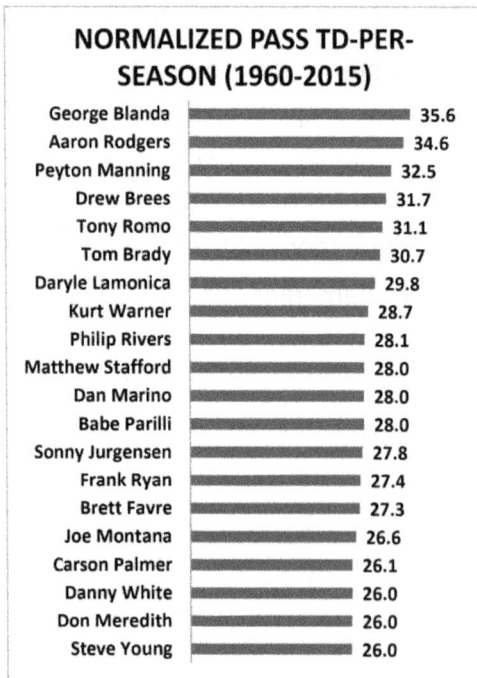

Figure 27 –Top 20 Normalized Yards and TDs per Season

NORMALIZED – INFLATION-ADJUSTED AVERAGE GAME X16

Inflation-adjusted accumulated career totals divided by the number of games started multiplied by 16 to output the equivalent of one full season

When we applied the inflation adjustment, the passing yards-per-season Top 10 does not change drastically from the previous non-adjusted list with seven repeated names – Warner, Brees, Stafford, Peyton, Rodgers, Schaub and Romo. The last three names in the Top 10 included Hogeboom, Marino and Fouts (Figure 28).

The same trend also occurs with the passing TDs. The top-10 remains mostly unchanged from the previous section – Rodgers, Peyton, Brees, Brady, Romo, Marino, Warner, Blanda, Favre and Stafford.

While a few more QBs from the 80s placed on this list, these QBs played in teams with pass-heavy offensive attacks. Undoubtedly, Marino and Fouts led the passing charge in the 80s, with both of them averaging more than 30 attempts per game for their career. But we will correct this bias in the next section to yield the best "adjusted and normalized" season.

NORMALIZED ADJUSTED PASS YARDS/SEASON (1960-2015)

Player	Yards
Kurt Warner	4,347
Drew Brees	4,327
Matthew Stafford	4,223
Peyton Manning	4,202
Aaron Rodgers	4,159
Matt Schaub	4,135
Tony Romo	4,118
Gary Hogeboom	4,108
Dan Marino	4,092
Dan Fouts	4,067
Wade Wilson	4,018
Tom Brady	3,999
Joe Montana	3,979
Philip Rivers	3,959
Steve Bono	3,956
Matt Ryan	3,946
Trent Green	3,943
George Blanda	3,933
Vince Evans	3,921
Ben Roethlisberger	3,900

NORMALIZED ADJUSTED PASS TD-PER-SEASON (1960-2015)

Player	TDs
Aaron Rodgers	39.6
Peyton Manning	38.9
Drew Brees	37.9
Tom Brady	36.6
Tony Romo	36.5
Dan Marino	35.6
Kurt Warner	35.4
George Blanda	34.9
Brett Favre	34.2
Matthew Stafford	33.7
Joe Montana	33.5
Philip Rivers	33.2
Daryle Lamonica	32.8
Steve Bono	32.5
Danny White	32.3
Steve Young	32.3
Carson Palmer	31.6
Randall Cunningham	31.5
Eli Manning	31.1
Mark Rypien	31.0

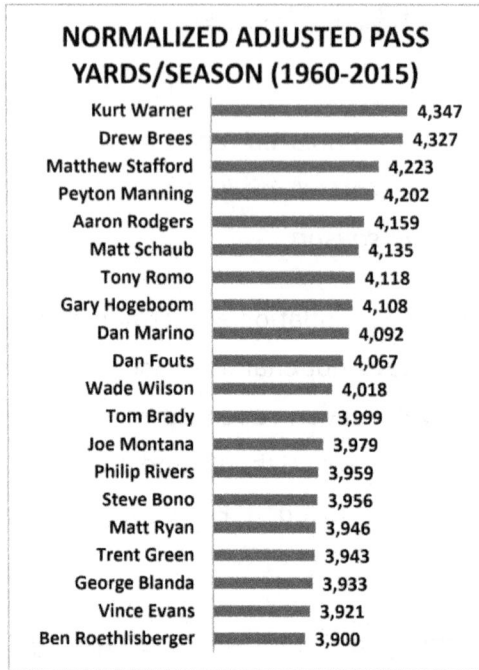

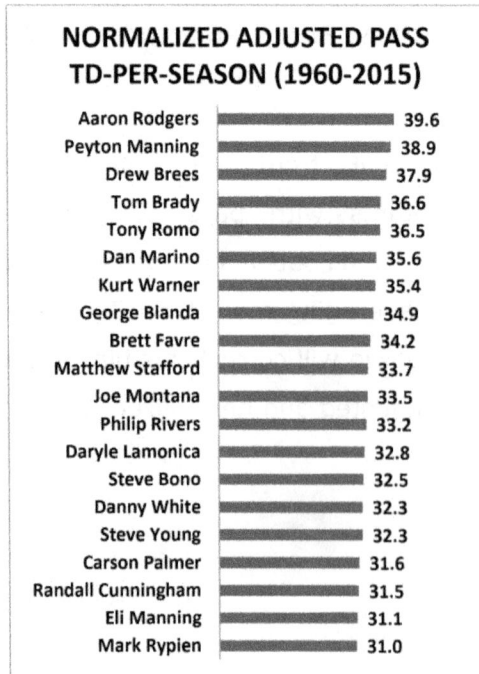

Figure 28 –Top 20 Normalized Yards and TDs per Season Adjusted

NORMALIZED – AVERAGE GAME (31 ATTEMPTS) X16

Inflation-adjusted accumulated career totals normalized to 31 attempts-per-game then multiplied by 16 to output the equivalent of one full season

When we applied the inflation adjustment *and* the normalizing for 31 attempts-per-game, the picture changed completely on both lists, resulting in a healthy smattering of names from the Modern Era (Figure 29). On the passing yards, Young jumps to the top spot followed by Berry, Starr, Morrall, Unitas and Staubach. Fouts and Warner, two Air Coryell specialists, make a strong appearance at sixth and seventh. Dawson and Jurgensen add two more names from the sixties into the Top 10. On the TD list, 60s QB F. Ryan sneaks by Rodgers, and they led the rest of the pack by more than two TDs per season. Young ranks third followed by Lamonica, Dawson, Peyton, Romo, Brady, White and Griese. Griese's name on the list, ahead of the likes of Marino, Montana and Warner, is quite surprising. However, the mark of the early 70's Dolphins was the pounding of Larry Csonka, Jim Kiick and Mercury Morris behind a talented offensive line of future Hall of Famers Jim Langer, Larry Little, and Bob Kuechenberg. Griese averaged only 363 passing attempts per season, which is dwarfed by today's offensive juggernauts attempting in excess of 600 passes per season.

These two lists with inflation-adjustment and pass attempt normalizing lend credibility to the quality of the QBs from the 60s and 70s. Their stats only became obsolete by the oncoming attempt inflation and changing style of the game. But, for sure, they could hold their own against the best from today.

NORMALIZED ADJUSTED PASS YARDS/SEASON (31 ATTEMPT)

Player	Yards
Steve Young	3,949
Bob Berry	3,928
Bart Starr	3,911
Earl Morrall	3,887
Johnny Unitas	3,866
Roger Staubach	3,850
Dan Fouts	3,847
Kurt Warner	3,841
Len Dawson	3,837
Aaron Rodgers	3,791
Sonny Jurgensen	3,776
Ben Roethlisberger	3,768
Joe Montana	3,753
Frank Ryan	3,749
Steve Grogan	3,748
Tony Romo	3,743
Lynn Dickey	3,740
Billy Wade	3,738
Craig Morton	3,731
Bill Nelsen	3,722

NORMALIZED ADJUSTED PASS TD/SEASON (31 ATTEMPT)

Player	TD
Frank Ryan	36.2
Aaron Rodgers	36.1
Steve Young	34.5
Daryle Lamonica	34.4
Len Dawson	34.4
Peyton Manning	34.1
Tony Romo	33.1
Tom Brady	32.5
Danny White	32.2
Bob Griese	32.1
Terry Bradshaw	32.1
Sonny Jurgensen	31.9
Dan Marino	31.6
Joe Montana	31.6
Earl Morrall	31.6
Jim Kelly	31.4
Drew Brees	31.4
Kurt Warner	31.3
Dave Krieg	31.1
Brett Favre	31.1

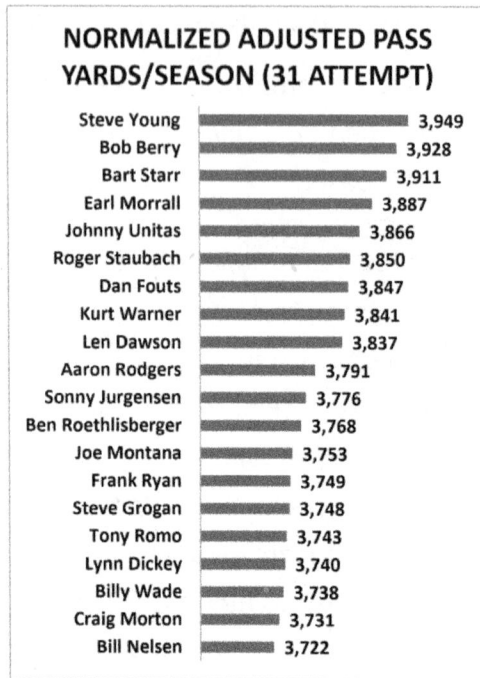

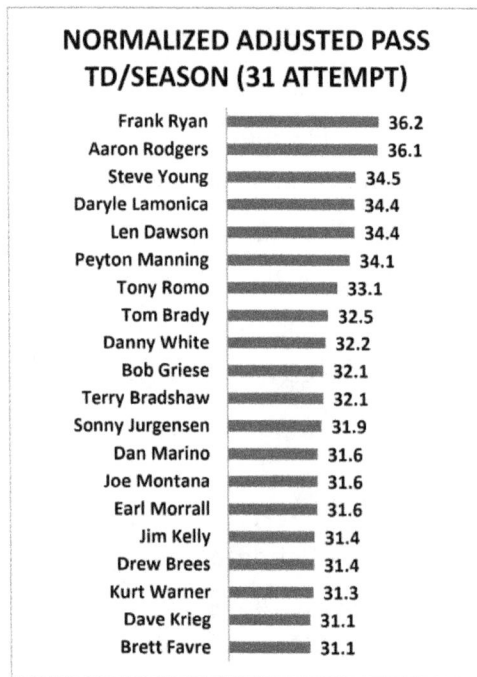

Figure 29 –Top 20 Normalized Yards & TDs per Season (31 Attempts)

THE BEST COMBINED SKILLS

Adjusting the modified QB rating (mQBR) for inflation, the chart below (Figure 30) shows the quarterbacks with the Best Combined Skills of passing, running, scrambling and sack avoidance.

Before we present the list, we need to address an issue with missing data. Even though the NFL started to record team sacks in 1961, the league did not track sacks and sack yards by QB until 1969. As a workaround, we estimated the missing sacks and sack yards for those years. We filled the blanks by extrapolating the sacks and sack yards as a percentage of the number of team pass attempts for each of those years. For example, if a team gave up 40 sacks and 200 sack yards, we gave each QB in the team a portion of the sacks and sack yards as a percentage of their pass attempts. If a QB attempted half of the team passes, then he would inherit 20 sacks and 100 sack yards. While not ideal, estimating the totals was preferable to ignoring the missing data, which would have dramatically improved the ranking of the QBs that played before 1969.

Peyton sits at the top of the list with the Best Combined Skills. Montana fills the number two spot. Old timers will swear by the name at number three, Jurgensen. Jurgensen led the league in passing yards and TDs routinely in the sixties. In fact, seven QBs from that era made the Top 20 – Jurgensen, Tarkenton, Lamonica, Dawson, Unitas, Brodie and Starr.

Young, who continues to impress with his strong showings, ranks fourth followed by Marino, Brees, Rodgers, Brady, Tarkenton and Anderson to close out the Top 10.

BEST COMBINED QB SKILLS ADJUSTED mQBR (1960-2015)

QB	mQBR
Peyton Manning	87.5
Joe Montana	87.3
Sonny Jurgensen	86.9
Steve Young	83.6
Dan Marino	83.2
Drew Brees	83.2
Aaron Rodgers	82.8
Tom Brady	81.4
Fran Tarkenton	80.8
Ken Anderson	80.6
Tony Romo	79.9
Roger Staubach	79.5
Daryle Lamonica	79.4
Bert Jones	79.3
Len Dawson	78.8
Johnny Unitas	78.7
John Brodie	78.7
Bart Starr	78.0
Dan Fouts	77.6
Philip Rivers	77.5

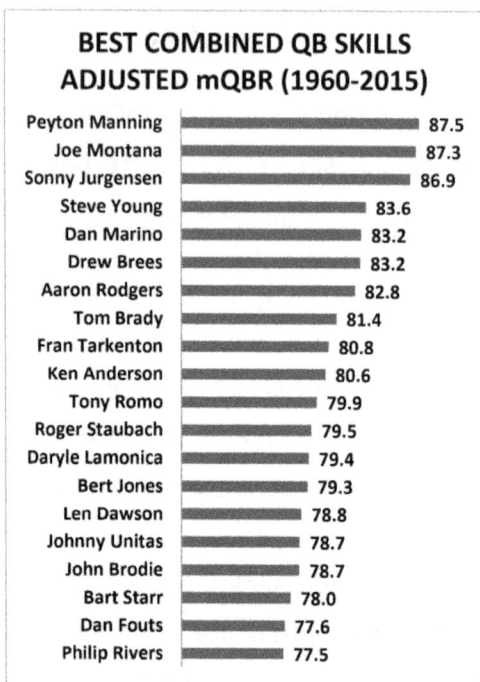

Figure 30 –Top 20 Inflation-Adjusted mQBR

A host of All-Time QBs filled the rest of the Top 20 with names like Staubach, Jones, Dawson, Unitas, Starr and Fouts. Romo and Rivers made a strong showing, breaking into the Top 20. Two names, though, that may have been expected to make the Several HOFers and great QBs just missed this list, placing in the next ten spots: Warner, Kelly, Griese, Favre and Aikman.

The Best Combined Skills account for the non-passing dimensions of the QB position and inflation adjustment. However, it does not account for one huge portion necessary to rank the All-Time greats – the "it" factor. The next section takes on the impact of a winning record on the QB rankings.

THE WINNINGEST

The NFL tracks statistics for just about every aspect of performance. After scrutinizing and correlating the relationship of the different available stats to winning, we decided on the win-loss records for the regular season, how far a QB took his team in the playoffs and game-winning drives to analyze and identify the winningest QB.

Before we begin the analysis, though, we need to discuss how the NFL playoff expansion has affected the postseason over the years. As with QB stat inflation, the playoff schedule has expanded five times since 1960. From 1960 to 1966, the NFL and AFL had two divisions, and the winner of each would meet to be crowned champion. There was only one playoff game played in each league until the winners of the NFL and AFL started interleague play in the Super Bowl in 1966.

The AFL maintained a two-team format until 1968 when they added a wildcard, which would play the lower seed of the two divisional winners, then a second wildcard in 1969.

After 1967, the NFL split their 16 teams into four divisions and expanded the playoff format to include the winners from each division. After the merger in 1970, each conference (AFC and NFC) had three division winners plus one wildcard as the number of playoff teams expanded to eight teams. In 1978, a second wildcard team was added to each conference so that ten teams reached the playoffs. In 1990, the playoffs were expanded again adding a third wildcard team per conference so that 12 teams made the postseason. In 2002, the NFL realigned the teams again from three to four divisions per conference, but the number of teams in the playoffs did not change, remaining at 12. In summary, in the last five decades, the number of playoff teams increased from four to twelve.

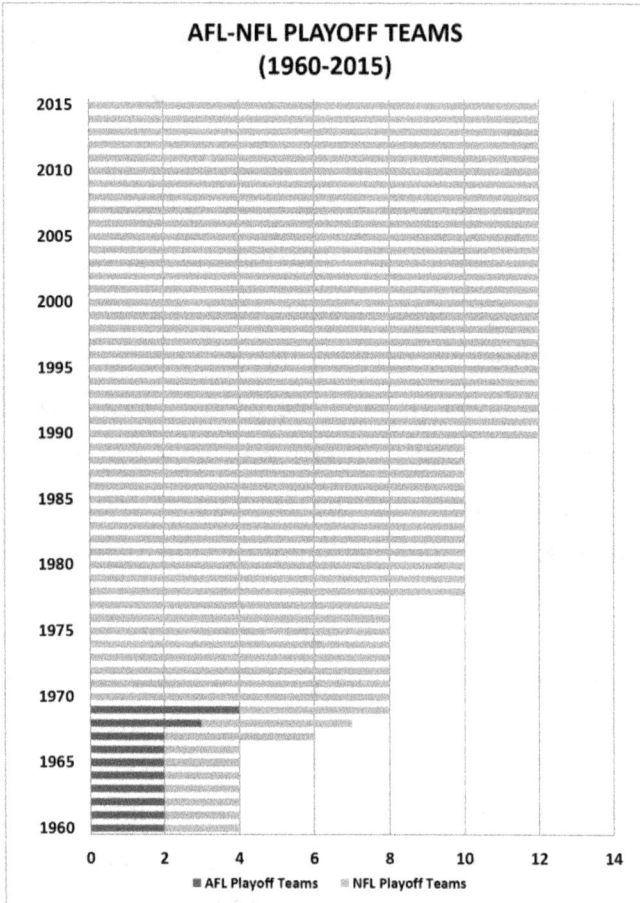

Figure 31 – Number of Playoff Teams per Year from 1960-2015

Why is the postseason expansion critical to the win metrics? Simple – more postseason games means more opportunities for stat accumulation but also for winning percentages gone astray. The career playoff leaders became a function of the expanded schedule – the players from the sixties and seventies did not stand a chance against the post-merger players. A player before 1966 only had one opportunity per season, whereas, after 1978 he had at least three, four if on a wildcard team. Quarterbacks on perennial playoff contending teams like Montana, Elway, Favre, Peyton and Brady have accumulated more than 20 playoff games each. Before 1978, few QBs would get the opportunity to play in as many as dozen postseason games for their entire career. The only exceptions were the Steelers and Cowboys dynasties, where Bradshaw and Staubach played in 19 and 17 playoff games, respectively.

REGULAR VS. POSTSEASON

The first thing that is evident when comparing regular season vs. postseason records is that there is no correlation between the two. Unless you win the Super Bowl, you are guaranteed one loss for every year that your team reaches the playoffs. This seems trivial and obvious, but it accounts for a huge disparity in playoff winning percentages because the losses mount quicker than the wins unless you are going deep into the playoffs every year. There is a glut of quarterbacks with winning regular season percentages but losing playoff records.

Also, if a QB is taking his teams to the playoffs regularly, but not going deep into the postseason, then he is pretty much guaranteed a losing percentage. The names Marino and Kelly come to mind. The Dolphins reached the playoffs in 10 of 17 years, but Miami did not win any SBs during that span. Marino managed to win at least one game in seven of those ten years but even then, his playoff record is a paltry 8-10 compared to his regular season record of 147-93. Similarly, Kelly led the Bills into the postseason in eight of 11 years, and even though reached the Super Bowl four times, his playoff record stands near .500, 9-8, as compared to a regular season of 101-59.

In the regular season, five QBs led the pack *winning over 70% of their games* – Lamonica, Brady, Staubach, Montana and Peyton (Figure 32). The top three quarterbacks averaged an impressive 12 wins per 16-game season for their teams. McMahon, Bradshaw, White, F. Ryan, Rodgers, Roethlisberger and Bono won more than two-thirds of their games.

For ranking the postseason winning percentage, we enforced an eight-game minimum to eliminate bizarre Dilferian stats to skew the data (Trent Dilfer owns a 5-1 postseason record with four of those wins coming in 2000, the year his wildcard Ravens won the Super Bowl). In the postseason, Starr (9-1), Plunkett (8-2), Unitas (6-2) and Theismann (6-2) own the best records in terms of winning percentages, but their opportunities were fewer than the other names on this list as each played ten or fewer games. Because of the limited opportunities in the 60s, as explained earlier, Starr only took his team to the playoffs in six of his 16 years – Plunkett and Theismann even less. Bradshaw, Aikman, Eli Manning and Brady scored the only other postseason percentages over 70%, while Montana and Warner just missed out, each with more than 69%.

If we sort the postseason records by the number of wins, only ten players enjoy double-digit wins, with Brady far in front with 22 wins. Montana won 16 games while Bradshaw, Elway and Peyton earned 14 each. Favre, Aikman, Staubach, Big Ben and Flacco made up the rest of the list with 10+ wins.

REGULAR SEASON WINNING PERCENTAGE (1960-2015)

Quarterback	Percentage
Daryle Lamonica	78.4%
Tom Brady	77.1%
Roger Staubach	74.6%
Joe Montana	71.3%
Peyton Manning	70.2%
Jim McMahon	69.1%
Terry Bradshaw	67.7%
Danny White	67.4%
Frank Ryan	67.2%
Aaron Rodgers	67.2%
Ben Roethlisberger	66.9%
Steve Bono	66.7%
Ken Stabler	66.1%
Steve Young	65.7%
Andy Dalton	65.6%
Bob Lee	65.5%
David Woodley	65.1%
Pat Haden	64.5%
Johnny Unitas	64.5%
Earl Morrall	64.5%

POSTSEASON WINNING PERCENTAGE (1960-2015)

Quarterback	Percentage
Bart Starr	90.0 %
Jim Plunkett	80.0 %
Joe Theismann	75.0 %
Johnny Unitas	75.0 %
Terry Bradshaw	73.7 %
Troy Aikman	73.3 %
Eli Manning	72.7 %
Tom Brady	71.0 %
Joe Montana	69.6 %
Kurt Warner	69.2 %
Joe Flacco	66.7 %
John Elway	66.7 %
Ben Roethlisberger	64.7 %
Roger Staubach	64.7 %
Jake Delhomme	62.5 %
Len Dawson	62.5 %
Phil Simms	60.0 %
Ken Stabler	58.3 %
Steve Young	57.1 %
Donovan McNabb	56.3 %

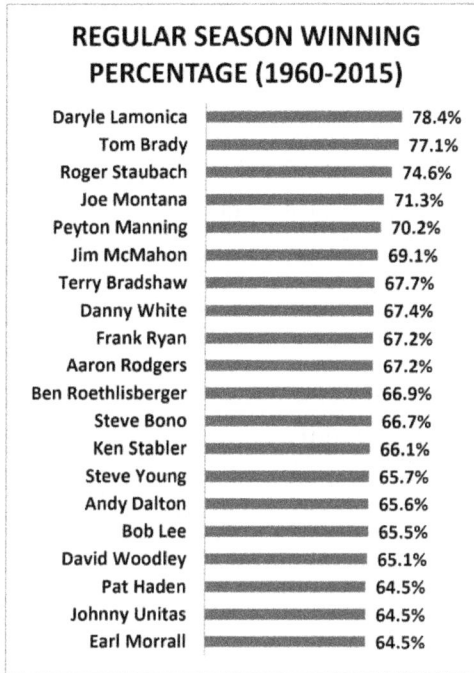

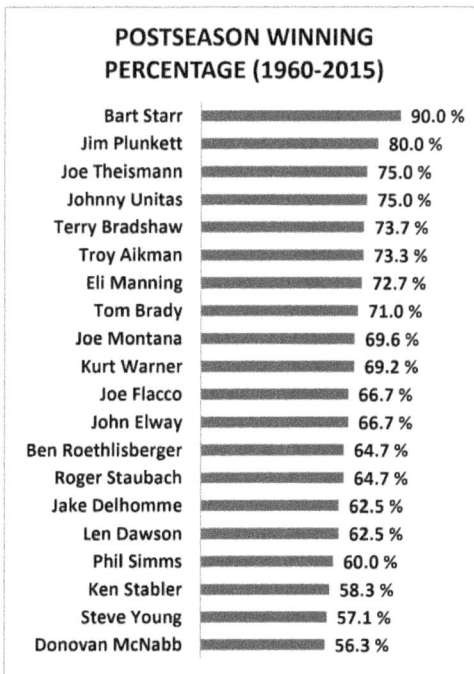

Figure 32 –Top 20 QB Regular & Postseason Winning Percentage

GAME-WINNING DRIVES

As with the Rose career hits leader analogy, the game-winning drives (GWD) totals can deceive when taken at face value. Players that played longer inherited more opportunities to accumulate stats. We presented the data as a total sum and as a percentage of total

In the charts below (Figure 33), Peyton tied for first with Brady in total game-winning drives (regular and postseason) with 57. His little brother Eli ranks ninth with 38, but when we factor the number of games played, Eli edges Peyton by a nose, 19.6% to 19.5%. Favre ranks fifth on the career total list with 47 GWDs, but does not crack the Top 20 on the per-game list due to having played over 300 career games. Notable old timers on both lists with reputations for comebacks included Tarkenton, Staubach, Unitas and Bradshaw.

Only Brady, Marino, Elway, Roethlisberger and Montana placed in the Top 10 of both lists. Delhomme, surprisingly, took the top spot on the per-game list with one game-winning drive per four starts in his career (25%). Matt Ryan came in second, lending credibility to his "Matty Ice" nickname. Romo impressed with his third place, one spot ahead of Brady – now, if he could only parlay that into some postseason hardware.

REGULAR + POSTSEASON
GAME WINNING DRIVES

Player	GWD
Tom Brady	57
Peyton Manning	57
Dan Marino	55
John Elway	52
Brett Favre	47
Drew Brees	41
Ben Roethlisberger	40
Warren Moon	39
Eli Manning	38
Joe Montana	38
Fran Tarkenton	35
Vinny Testaverde	33
Matt Ryan	32
Johnny Unitas	31
Terry Bradshaw	31
Drew Bledsoe	31
Tony Romo	31
Jim Kelly	30
Kerry Collins	30
Jake Plummer	30

REGULAR + POSTSEASON
GWD-PER-GAME

Player	Per-Game
Jake Delhomme	25.0%
Matt Ryan	24.4%
Tony Romo	23.7%
Tom Brady	22.4%
Ben Roethlisberger	21.5%
Dan Marino	21.3%
Jake Plummer	21.1%
John Elway	20.6%
Brad Johnson	20.5%
Joe Montana	20.3%
Joe Theismann	19.7%
Eli Manning	19.6%
Peyton Manning	19.5%
Randall Cunningham	19.4%
Roger Staubach	19.1%
Joe Flacco	19.0%
Carson Palmer	18.6%
Jay Cutler	18.4%
Ken Stabler	18.4%
Warren Moon	18.3%

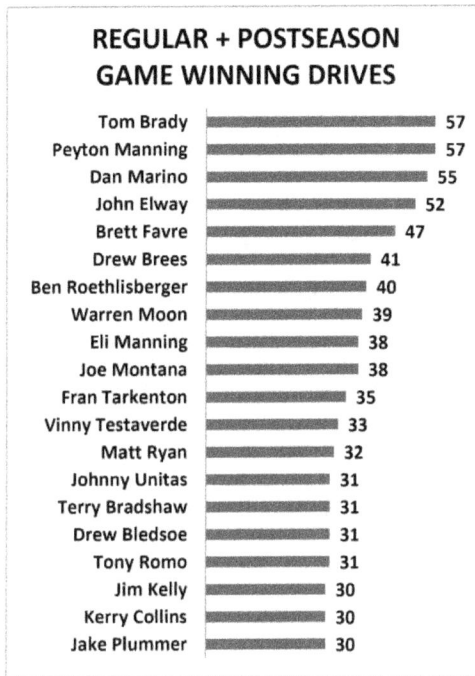

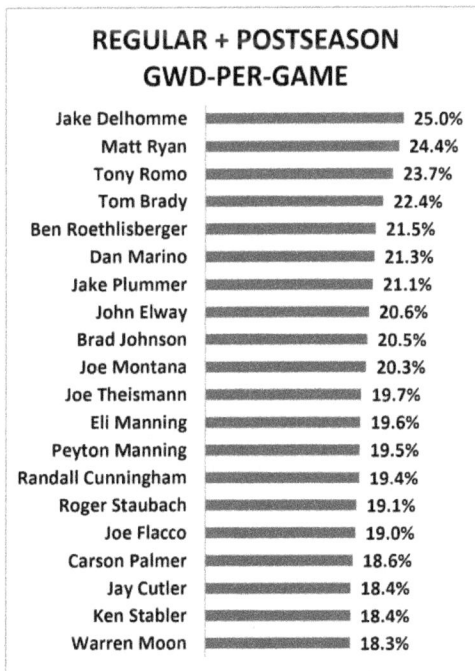

Figure 33 –Top 20 Regular & Postseason GWD and Per-Game

POSTSEASON APPEARANCES

There is no better case study for the impact of a quarterback leading his team to the playoffs than Peyton Manning and the Indianapolis Colts. Coming into the 2011 season, Indy had made the playoffs a record ten straight times. When Peyton missed the entire season due to a neck injury, the Colts dropped to a dismal 2-14 record. After averaging more than 12 wins per season for the previous ten, virtually the same team sans Peyton won only two.

Football is a team sport and unlike basketball, in which one player can carry a team, even a great quarterback can only take them so far. A porous defense is the Achilles heel of any team sport but is particularly the case in football. An elite quarterback can get you to the postseason but to close the deal, he needs a decent supporting cast. Consequently, the number of times that a starting quarterback leads his team to the playoffs is a great indicator of his worth. The list below (Figure 34) is a very exclusive club since only 25 of all the qualifying QBs led their team to the postseason more than 50%.

Peyton, Rodgers, Brady, Staubach and Dalton sit at the top, leading their teams to the postseason more than 80% of the time (although Dalton's sample size is small at only five seasons) Montana, Flacco, Kemp and Kelly reached the postseason more than 70% of the time. Roethlisberger, Bradshaw, Favre and Newton made it at least 60% of the time. Again, it was surprising to see Big Ben so high on this list and especially that he upstaged another Steelers great – Bradshaw. The last group at greater than 50% included Marino, Aikman, Elway, White, McNabb, Griese, Williams, Ferragamo, Lamonica, Haden, Rivers and Ryan. It is worth mentioning that no quarterbacks from the sixties, other than Lamonica, made this list. It was disappointing to find that all-time greats Starr, Dawson and Unitas only led their teams to the playoffs about a third of the time. Also, Jurgensen never made the playoffs as a starting QB in his entire career. However, there is a reason for this. Remember that the playoff format before 1966 only sent the winner of each division to the Championship Game. If their team came in second in their division, they got zero credit. Fast-forward a few years and that same second place team played at least a wildcard game.

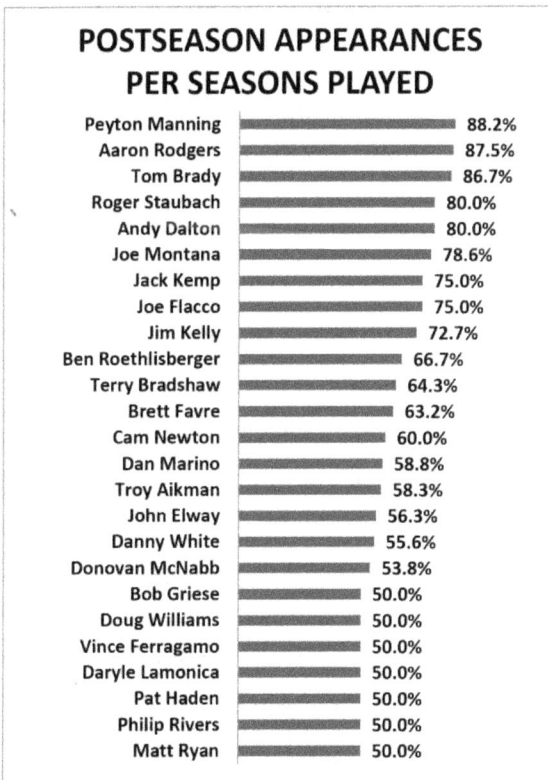

POSTSEASON APPEARANCES PER SEASONS PLAYED

Quarterback	Percentage
Peyton Manning	88.2%
Aaron Rodgers	87.5%
Tom Brady	86.7%
Roger Staubach	80.0%
Andy Dalton	80.0%
Joe Montana	78.6%
Jack Kemp	75.0%
Joe Flacco	75.0%
Jim Kelly	72.7%
Ben Roethlisberger	66.7%
Terry Bradshaw	64.3%
Brett Favre	63.2%
Cam Newton	60.0%
Dan Marino	58.8%
Troy Aikman	58.3%
John Elway	56.3%
Danny White	55.6%
Donovan McNabb	53.8%
Bob Griese	50.0%
Doug Williams	50.0%
Vince Ferragamo	50.0%
Daryle Lamonica	50.0%
Pat Haden	50.0%
Philip Rivers	50.0%
Matt Ryan	50.0%

Figure 34 –Top 20 Postseason Appearances per Seasons Played

JUST WIN, BABY!

"Super Bowl wins is the only metric that matters to distinguish an elite quarterback!" This is the absurd argument that Trent Dilfer is a better quarterback than Dan Fouts or Dan Marino. Or that Eli is better than Peyton because he owns more rings (pre 2015). Or even more ridiculous, that Eli is better than Brady because he beat Tom twice in head-to-head Super Bowls. The Eli-Peyton argument is so insane that we dedicated a section exclusively to the Mannings in the Bonus Morsels chapter.

Breaking down the SB winning quarterbacks, one-hit wonders littered the list. Rypien, Hostetler, Williams, Dilfer and Johnson sounds more like a hippie band from the early seventies than a list of SB winners. Other, more respectable, one-time winners include Namath, Stabler, Simms, Theismann and Rodgers.

When we compiled the list of QBs with multiple championship wins (AFL and NFL), the list narrowed quickly. Kemp, Blanda, Rote, Dawson, Staubach, Griese, Plunkett, Elway, Peyton, Roethlisberger and Eli won two each. Unitas and Aikman each collected three Lombardi trophies. *Bradshaw, Montana and Brady have four apiece and Starr leads the pack with five.*

If we sort by championship appearances, Aikman, Dawson, Rote, Griese, Roethlisberger, Warner and Tarkenton played in three games with various levels of success – Aikman won three and Tarkenton lost three. Bradshaw, Montana, Unitas, Blanda, Staubach, Peyton and Kelly participated in four each. Bradshaw and Montana won all of their opportunities while Kelly struck out. Kemp and Elway each played in five, winning two. Finally, Starr and Brady led their teams to six championship games, winning five and four, respectively.

Note that all the championship quarterbacks with multiple appearances, except for Morton, ranked in at least one of the Top 20 Best QB lists, which makes a good case for a high correlation between elite QB play and championships.

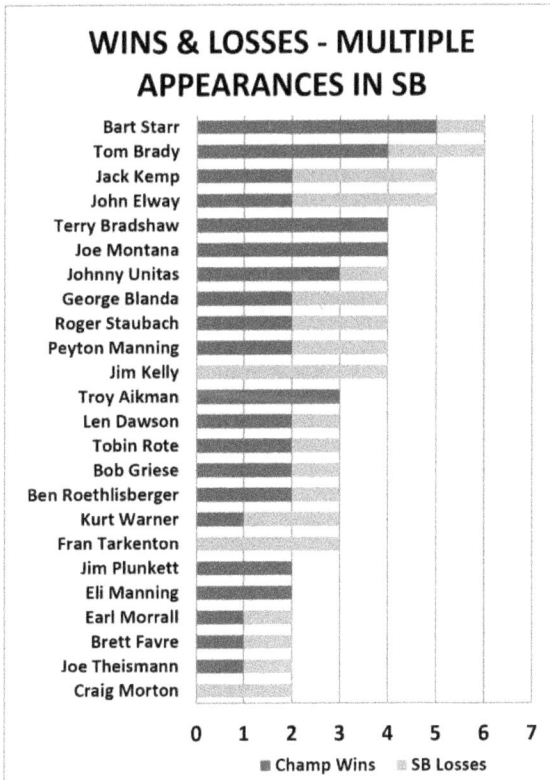

WINS & LOSSES - MULTIPLE APPEARANCES IN SB

	Champ Wins	SB Losses
Bart Starr		
Tom Brady		
Jack Kemp		
John Elway		
Terry Bradshaw		
Joe Montana		
Johnny Unitas		
George Blanda		
Roger Staubach		
Peyton Manning		
Jim Kelly		
Troy Aikman		
Len Dawson		
Tobin Rote		
Bob Griese		
Ben Roethlisberger		
Kurt Warner		
Fran Tarkenton		
Jim Plunkett		
Eli Manning		
Earl Morrall		
Brett Favre		
Joe Theismann		
Craig Morton		

Figure 35 –List of Championship QBs with Multiple Appearances

QB Win Rating (QBWR)

To determine the winningest quarterback, we developed a measurement method that combined three different aspects of winning. This metric accounted for regular season wins, game-winning drives and postseason success. More importantly, we weighed the pieces according to their individual worth. By order of importance, the regular season was less important than game-winning drives, which in turn was less important than postseason success. Also, we calibrated the value of the postseason by how deep each QB took his team – winning in the wildcard, divisional, conference and the SB games gained progressively increasing value.

To summarize, we defined the QB win rating (QBWR) metric as the combination of these three ingredients:

- Regular season winning percentage
- Game-winning drives (regular and postseason)
- Postseason win metric (not postseason winning percentage*)

* We chose not to use the postseason winning percentage because it was too volatile as explained earlier, so instead, we defined a postseason metric as a weighted scale awarding progressive value for reaching the playoffs, moving to the divisional round, winning the conference and winning the SB.

Before presenting the QBWR results, one additional fine-tuning needs explanation. Because of the lack of postseason opportunities discussed previously, the players from the sixties were severely handicapped in the QBWR rating. They only received one win for a championship, whereas, after 1967, the SB winning team would have earned three, and up to four wins if they had been a wildcard team after 1978. This was highly unfair, so we fudged a compensation factor to their playoff win total to level the playing field. Before 1967, we awarded the SB winning QBs 2.5 playoff wins to equalize them with the post-1967 format. This adjustment worked well as players such Starr, Unitas and Dawson moved up the list to their rightful place.

The final order of the QBWR list (Figure 36) did not surprise as every one of the Top 20 QBs won at least one championship.

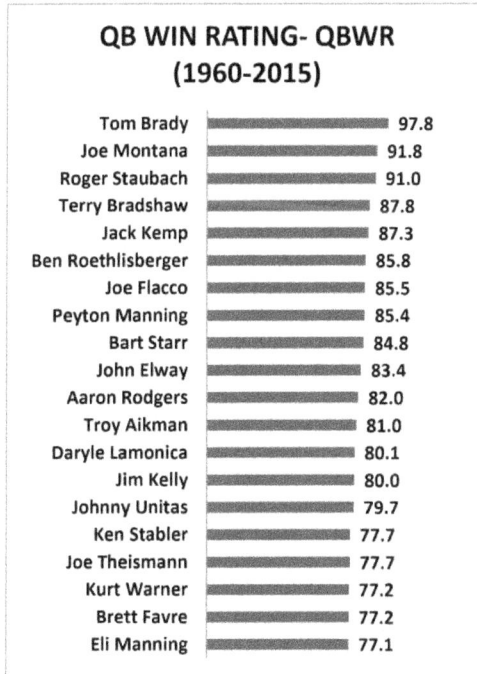

QB WIN RATING- QBWR (1960-2015)

Tom Brady	97.8
Joe Montana	91.8
Roger Staubach	91.0
Terry Bradshaw	87.8
Jack Kemp	87.3
Ben Roethlisberger	85.8
Joe Flacco	85.5
Peyton Manning	85.4
Bart Starr	84.8
John Elway	83.4
Aaron Rodgers	82.0
Troy Aikman	81.0
Daryle Lamonica	80.1
Jim Kelly	80.0
Johnny Unitas	79.7
Ken Stabler	77.7
Joe Theismann	77.7
Kurt Warner	77.2
Brett Favre	77.2
Eli Manning	77.1

Figure 36 – Top 20 QB Win Rating Metric, QBWR

Perennial contenders and multiple champions Brady, Montana, Staubach, Bradshaw and Kemp led the list. Even though Bradshaw owned more SB rings, Staubach outperformed him due to higher metrics in regular season wins and game-winning drives.

Roethlisberger ranks sixth on this list and continues to place highly on some very impressive lists. Flacco and his postseason winning ways pushed him up to #7 on the list, one spot ahead of Peyton, who helped his case with a second SB ring in 2015. Starr slides in at number nine on the strength of his five championships. By the way, without the adjustment, Starr would not have placed in the Top 20, surely a travesty. Elway placed tenth, as the two SB wins at the end of his career boosted his placement.

Rodgers placed tenth, and Aikman 11th as his three rings pushed him up the list. Lamonica and his category-leading regular season win percentage landed him at #12. It was pleasing to see Kelly place 13th on this list. Getting his team to the playoffs in eight of 11 seasons and the SB four years in a row is a testament to his resilience and toughness. As mentioned earlier, the fact that he did not win any SBs speaks to the inability of his team to get over the hump or kick a FG two more feet to the left.

At 14th, Unitas earned just reward for three rings in four appearances. Stabler, Theismann, Warner and Favre bunched together, all with one SB win. Eli posted the last spot on the Top 20. While Eli may own two rings, his inconsistent QB play continues to hold him back, as his Giants have made the postseason less than half of the time.

THE BEST EVER

Now that we identified the best performers by category in the previous chapters, the focus will narrow to the Best Ever.

TOTAL QB RATING (tQBR)

As discussed previously, the Best Ever ranking and rating needed to account for stat inflation, missing dimensions of QB play and winning record. We defined this new metric, the total QB rating, tQBR, by combining the inflation-adjusted mQBR and the QBWR to rank and rate the field.

Before presenting the Best Ever, let us summarize the Top 20 quarterbacks by category. Note that we highlighted HOFers in gray and new additions since the First Edition of this book in bold italics.

TOP QBs BY SUB-CATEGORY

No	Best Runner	Least Sacked	Best Season
1	Michael Vick	Peyton Manning	Milt Plum - 1960
2	Bobby Douglass	Dan Marino	Peyton Manning - 2004
3	Randall Cunningham	Doug Williams	Bart Starr - 1966
4	Greg Landry	George Blanda	Roger Staubach - 1971
5	Mike Pagel	Mark Rypien	Y.A. Tittle - 1963
6	Virgil Carter	Drew Brees	Joe Montana - 1989
7	Steve Young	Steve Bono	Ken Stabler - 1976
8	Bert Jones	Joe Namath	Aaron Rodgers - 2011
9	Archie Manning	Matt Ryan	Steve Young - 1994
10	Fran Tarkenton	Mike Tomczak	Bert Jones - 1976
11	Donovan McNabb	Joey Harrington	Len Dawson - 1966
12	Ken Anderson	Jeff Garcia	Dan Marino - 1984
13	Roger Staubach	Derek Anderson	Tom Brady - 2007
14	John Brodie	Eli Manning	Len Dawson - 1968
15	Steve McNair	Doug Flutie	Nick Foles - 2013
16	Cam Newton	Carson Palmer	Len Dawson - 1962
17	Vince Evans	Tom Brady	Steve Young - 1992
18	Bart Starr	Brett Favre	Johnny Unitas - 1965
19	Marty Domres	Kerry Collins	Bart Starr - 1964
20	Daunte Culpepper	Mark Malone	Kurt Warner - 1999

TOP QBs BY NORMALIZED SEASON

No	Most Yards	Most TDs	Least Interceptions
1	Steve Young	Frank Ryan	Roman Gabriel
2	Bob Berry	Aaron Rodgers	Bart Starr
3	Bart Starr	Steve Young	Joe Montana
4	Earl Morrall	Daryle Lamonica	Virgil Carter
5	Johnny Unitas	Len Dawson	Neil O'Donnell
6	Roger Staubach	Peyton Manning	Bill Munson
7	Dan Fouts	Tony Romo	Sonny Jurgensen
8	Kurt Warner	Tom Brady	Neil Lomax
9	Len Dawson	Danny White	Fran Tarkenton
10	Aaron Rodgers	Bob Griese	Bernie Kosar
11	Sonny Jurgensen	Terry Bradshaw	Ken O'Brien
12	Ben Roethlisberger	Sonny Jurgensen	Roger Staubach
13	Joe Montana	Dan Marino	Aaron Rodgers
14	Frank Ryan	Joe Montana	Ken Anderson
15	Steve Grogan	Earl Morrall	Don Meredith
16	Tony Romo	Jim Kelly	Johnny Unitas
17	Lynn Dickey	Drew Brees	Steve Bono
18	Billy Wade	Kurt Warner	Steve Young
19	Craig Morton	Dave Krieg	Tony Eason
20	Bill Nelsen	Brett Favre	Tom Brady

TOP QBs BY aQBPR, mQBR AND QBWR

No	aQBPR	mQBR	QBWR
1	Steve Young	Peyton Manning	Tom Brady
2	Aaron Rodgers	Joe Montana	Joe Montana
3	Joe Montana	Sonny Jurgensen	Roger Staubach
4	Len Dawson	Steve Young	Terry Bradshaw
5	Sonny Jurgensen	Dan Marino	*Jack Kemp*
6	Roger Staubach	Drew Brees	Ben Roethlisberger
7	Bart Starr	Aaron Rodgers	*Joe Flacco*
8	Fran Tarkenton	Tom Brady	Peyton Manning
9	Peyton Manning	Fran Tarkenton	Bart Starr
10	Tom Brady	Ken Anderson	John Elway
11	Kurt Warner	Tony Romo	Aaron Rodgers
12	Ken Anderson	Roger Staubach	Troy Aikman
13	Tony Romo	*Daryle Lamonica*	*Daryle Lamonica*
14	Johnny Unitas	Bert Jones	Jim Kelly
15	*Frank Ryan*	Len Dawson	George Blanda
16	Drew Brees	Johnny Unitas	Johnny Unitas
17	*Bob Berry*	John Brodie	Ken Stabler
18	Dan Marino	Bart Starr	Joe Theismann
19	Philip Rivers	Dan Fouts	Kurt Warner
20	Bob Griese	Philip Rivers	Brett Favre
21	Earl Morrall	Kurt Warner	Eli Manning
22	Bert Jones	Jim Kelly	Danny White
23	Ben Roethlisberger	Bob Griese	Mark Rypien
24	Jim Kelly	*Matt Ryan*	Jim McMahon
25	Don Meredith	*Milt Plum*	Bob Griese

The Top 20 – Best Ever QBs

Here are the rankings for the Top 20 quarterbacks of the modern era. Brady and Montana sit at the top separated by 4 points from the rest of the field. Since the First Edition published in 2014, two new names made the list, Daryle Lamonica and Joe Flacco, which bumped Griese and Stabler into the #21 and #22 positions, respectively.

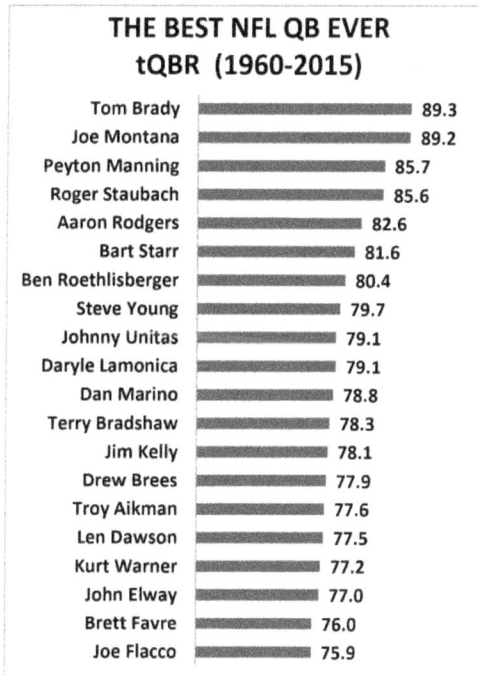

THE BEST NFL QB EVER
tQBR (1960-2015)

Quarterback	tQBR
Tom Brady	89.3
Joe Montana	89.2
Peyton Manning	85.7
Roger Staubach	85.6
Aaron Rodgers	82.6
Bart Starr	81.6
Ben Roethlisberger	80.4
Steve Young	79.7
Johnny Unitas	79.1
Daryle Lamonica	79.1
Dan Marino	78.8
Terry Bradshaw	78.3
Jim Kelly	78.1
Drew Brees	77.9
Troy Aikman	77.6
Len Dawson	77.5
Kurt Warner	77.2
John Elway	77.0
Brett Favre	76.0
Joe Flacco	75.9

Figure 37 –The Best QB Ever

1. *Tom Brady ranked as the Best Ever*. He combined Top 10 QB skills with, by far, the highest win rating. Brady's drive to make those around him better and to make no excuses is unparalleled. Shortly after his arrival in Foxboro, the Patriots became perennial contenders. Brady leapfrogged into the number one spot after the 2014 season by earning

his fourth Super Bowl ring in six attempts. Only Bart Starr has more championship rings. He also tied Montana with three SB MVP awards in 2015.

2. Joe Montana stepped down to the second position in 2014 after holding on to the top spot for over 20 years. Under the Bill Walsh's West Coast Offense, he redefined the quarterback position in the eighties. His most impressive stats were four SB appearances, four SB wins and three SB MVPs. He also ranked third in aQBPR, second in mQBR and second in QBWR. Montana was not only the coolest under pressure but also the best until Brady took over the top spot.

3. Peyton Manning squeaked past Staubach into third with his second SB in 2015. He also claimed the "most cerebral play caller ever" along with the best QB combined-skills. The Canton Club already started preparing his bust.

4. Roger Staubach slides one spot into fourth on the strength of his passing ability, scrambling, winning record, and SB rings. The Navy man rated strongly in the aQBPR, mQBR and QBWR lists at sixth, twelfth and third, respectively.

5. Aaron Rodgers is the next great passer QB on this list coming in at fifth. Rodgers' accuracy, touchdown-to-interception ratio and uncanny ability for not turning the ball over are unparalleled. He has an accomplished resume in only eight years as the starter in Green Bay after backing up Favre for the first three. Rodgers placed in the top of the aQBPR (2nd), mQBR (7th) and QBWR (11th) lists. He is

still in his prime and with a couple more Lombardi trophies on his resume, he could move up several spots on this list.

6. Bart Starr, reinforced by his five championships, came at #6. The passing skills and efficiency of Starr often went unnoticed because of the famed running attack of the Lombardi Packers. He never reached 300 passing attempts in a season, yet led the NFL in passing three times during the sixties. In addition to his outstanding 1966 campaign, which ranked as the third Best Season Ever, he had two other campaigns that would have ranked in the Top 10, but did not qualify due to lack of attempts.

7. Ben Roethlisberger sneaks into the number seven spot – his winning ways and consistently high performances across all metrics continue to push him up the relevant charts related to winning. Still in his prime, he has already played in three SBs, winning two. Even though he has won less SBs to date, he already passed over Pittsburgh legend Bradshaw on the strength of his passing skills.

8. Steve Young, at eighth, took the reins from Montana, and the 49ers never skipped a beat. For the next eight years, he was the best quarterback in the league with a passing efficiency never seen in the NFL, ranking first in overall aQBPR and fourth in mQBR.

9. Johnny Unitas placement at #9 did not surprise. His combination of passing ability and winning record supported his ranking on this list. He passed for over 40,000 yards, almost 300 TDs and threw a TD in 47 straight games, a mark that stood for over 50 years. His career

numbers were so far ahead of his time that he still ranks favorably even without inflation adjustments.

10. Daryle Lamonica snuck into the Top 10 on the strength of his 78% regular season winning percentage and strong performance in the modified metrics. The Mad Bomber became the perfect QB for Al Davis Vertical offense – a big QB with a strong accurate arm that could connect on the long ball. We inadvertently left Daryle off the first list in the First Edition – our apologies.

11. Dan Marino ranked 11th. When he reached the SB in his second year, after a monster 1984 season, he must have thought how effortless it was to advance to the dance. Sadly, he never made it past the AFC Championship game again. Shula could build neither a running game nor enough of a defensive team around him to win the big game.

12. Terry Bradshaw moved into the 12th spot, taking credit for the success of the Steelers dynasty of the seventies, even though he ranked poorly on the QB skills list. Give him credit, though, as he closed the deal all four times his Steelers made it to the championship game, playing well in the postseason each time and winning two SB MVP awards.

13. Jim Kelly placed #13 on the strength of his passing ability and winning record in spite of losing four SBs. The toughest hombre of the trio of Elway, Kelly and Marino, they will always be connected to the great QB draft of 1983. It is appropriate that all three placed in the Top 20 and landed in the HOF.

14. Drew Brees came in 14th. After a shoulder injury in 2005, his career was in question. Having another very promising QB already in Philip Rivers, the San Diego Chargers did not pursue Brees, and he signed with New Orleans Saints as a free agent that year. Under the tutelage of Sean Peyton and his pass-happy offense, Brees flourished into an elite QB. Along the way, he earned a SB ring and accumulated some very impressive career totals. He will be in Canton someday, possibly on the first ballot depending on the last few chapters of his career.

15. Troy Aikman, the other Cowboys legend, ranked #15. A third of The Triplets, along with Emmitt Smith and Michael Irvin, Troy led the Cowboys' resurgence in the nineties, and under his leadership, the Cowboys won three SBs. Perhaps the 'Boys would have won more, had Johnson and Jones learned to play nice.

16. At #16, Len Dawson won four AFL passing titles in ten years, leading the Kansas City Chiefs to three AFL championships. He made two SB appearances, winning the second one against the Minnesota Vikings and putting the final nail in the AFL-NFL merger.

17. Kurt Warner ranked 17th. He made the most of his chance in the NFL after working his way up the Arena and European Football leagues. Kurt then led the "Greatest Show on Turf" relentless attack of the St. Louis Rams, winning the SB and MVP honors in 1999. He later revived his career, leading the Arizona Cardinals to the 2008 SB and coming up just short of another win. A HOF finalist in 2015, Warner stands

as one of the most accurate passers ever and should make it into the HOF in 2016.

18. John Elway, at 18th, built a reputation as a clutch player when he led the Broncos on the famed 98-yard drive in the 1987 AFC Championship game against the Browns. While he owned the worst QB stats of the 1983 class, ranking 58th in aQBPR and 65th in mQBR, he was a winner throughout his career, leading the Broncos to five SBs. When Shanahan drafted Terrell Davis in the sixth round of the '95 draft, Elway had the final piece he needed. He finished his career with two SB wins and one SB MVP trophy that cemented his entrance into the Hall of Fame.

19. At 19th, Brett Favre, the ironman of the NFL, won one SB in two trips and held numerous career records due to his long, productive and injury free career (until recently when Peyton eclipsed just about every mark in the record book). Deservedly so, he joined the list of first-ballot Hall of Famers in 2016.

20. Joe Flacco worked his way into the mix at #20, carried by his seventh rank in win rating. His regular season passing metrics, however, paled in comparison, ranking below average in both aQBPR and mQBR. Joe still has plenty of career left in front of him, and it will be interesting to see if he already peaked or if he has more elite play left in him.

HONORABLE MENTIONS

- At #21, Bob Griese's entrance into the Hall of Fame came into question by some. His puny career totals stacked up poorly as compared to some of his contemporaries, then dwarfed by his eventual successor in Miami, Marino. However, when we took into account the style of offense of his early 70's Dolphins and normalized his passing skills, he fared very favorably against other HOF quarterbacks. He also led the Dolphins to three SBs, winning two including the only undefeated season in the history of the NFL.

- Ken "The Snake" Stabler led the John Madden Oakland Raiders in the seventies and ranked #22. He was a scrappy player that always did enough to win the game, even if not always pretty. His memorable shot-put toss to RB Clarence Davis in the end zone while dragged to the ground, dubbed "The Sea of Hands," closed the door on Miami's three-peat effort in 1974. In 1976, Stabler played an unbelievably productive season with a QBPR rating of 103.4 and leading the Raiders to their first SB win. That campaign ranked seventh on the list of the Best Season Ever by a QB. In 1978, his "Holy Roller" fumble changed the rules for recovering turnovers in the last two minutes of a game. Sadly, Ken Stabler died of cancer in 2015. The Senior Committee finally inducted him into HOF, posthumously, in 2016.

- Redskins' quarterbacks Theismann and Rypien impressed, placing 24th and 26th. Theismann comes up often on the HOF borderline list of hopefuls, but has not been able to garner enough support due to lean career totals. Rypien, on the other hand, enjoyed several very productive years in Washington then inexplicably disappeared, becoming a backup the rest of his career.

- It seemed appropriate that the Cowboys Tony Romo and Danny White landed so close to each other at #23 and #25. Their careers mirrored each other's so far – both stood as statistically elite quarterbacks that could not lead their teams deep into the postseason. The jury is still out on Romo, though, and if he could get some defensive help, he might just get over the hump.

- Rivers placed 28th, exposing the poor choice the Chargers made in taking him over Brees (14th). It is fitting that Rivers rated near White and Romo. This threesome leads the category of terrific Fantasy League players that have not delivered championships.

- Dan Fouts placed 40th, which speaks to the crap defensive teams he led his entire career. His adjusted mQBR rated a studly 19th, but he drops 21 spots in the tQBR on the weakness of his 84th ranking in winning record (QBWR).

- Donovan McNabb intrigued with his placement at 35th. While he enjoyed some very productive seasons with Coach Andy Reid in Philadelphia, he rated slightly above average in aQBPR (64th) and mQBR (74th). His winning record, four back-to-back trips to the NFC Championship game, along with his 29th place in QBWR lifted him in his overall rank.

- At #38, underrated Ken Anderson was a heck of a quarterback, as his 12th ranking in aQBPR and 10th in mQBR showed. In the strike-shortened year of 1982, he became the first QB ever to complete more than 70% of his passes in a season. His QBWR, however, dragged him down with a below average score (105th).

- Sonny Jurgensen plastered his name all over the best passer lists, ranking fifth in aQBPR and third in mQBR. His 157th ranking in QBWR, due to never playing a postseason game as the starter, however, dropped him to a pedestrian 43rd on this list.

- Another pair of QBs from the NFC East also rated similarly – Jeff Hostetler (#45) and Phil Simms (#60). Both scored above average values for aQBPR, mQBR and QBWR, but, more importantly, each brought home one Lombardi Trophy to NY.

- George Blanda came in at #50. We left him off the First Edition since he started playing in the NFL before the Korean War. He, however, played eight years as starting QB in the AFL, so we included him in this edition. He made the HOF on the strength of his arm and foot, playing until the ripe almost AARP age of 48, mostly kicking FGs for the last ten year.

- Matt Schaub's stock dropped like a rock to 51st once we exposed his inflated QBPR and poor winning record.

- Under Ted Marchibroda's Run & Gun offensive system, Bert Jones had a three-year run from 1975 to 1977 where he ranked among the elite QBs in the NFL. His 1976 campaign rated as the 10th Best Season Ever. However, he suffered a shoulder injury in 1978, never to recover his old form, which dropped him to #54 overall.

- Outside of delivering on his brash prediction and delivering the first ever 4,000 passing yard season, Broadway Joe Namath did not own stellar QB metrics and rated a highly unexpected 61st on our list. He did, however, earn an auspicious award in our Bonus Morsels.

- Warren Moon also surprised with his 67th place finish. His metrics rated slightly above average across the board, leaving us to wonder what could have been had he not wasted most of his prime in the CFL.

- Milt Plum, the object of one of the Bonus Morsels chapters, placed #74. He racked up decent aQBPR and mQBR scores at 36th and 25th, respectively, but his below average win metric held him back from joining the elite QBs of his time (Starr, Unitas, Blanda and Dawson).

- Daunte Culpepper also fell into the "sinking rock" category landing at #110. He enjoyed some early success, including one of the Top 10 Best Seasons, but only because he tossed the rock to The Freak, Randy Moss, in Minnesota.

- Papa Archie Manning scored a woeful 59.7 in tQBR, ranking 171st. His zero postseason appearances killed his QBWR and his overall value.

BONUS MORSELS

This section contains a series of unrelated essays on different QB related subjects.   There is no rhyme or reason as to the selection of these topics other than we found them interesting.

THE FAVRE ACCUMULATION EFFECT

Everybody knows that Favre was the career leader in passing yards and touchdowns (at the time of this writing Peyton was in the process of erasing all of Brett's records). However, is he the Best Ever?

Favre's biggest accomplishment is that he played twenty years relatively injury free, thereby accumulating gobs of yards, touchdowns and interceptions. However, when we normalized his statistics into a "per game" metric, he dropped to the bottom of the Top 20 Best Ever QBs. Much like Rose, Favre deserves credit as an aberration of accumulation. However, he was not the best passer in terms of efficiency or accuracy. He only broke the 100.0 QBPR level once in his career, and his QB passer rating had a pedestrian average of 86.0. Moreover, his gun-slinging ways seemed to yield a pick-six at the worst possible moment, especially towards the end of his career. He was, however, very consistent logging a QBPR rating under 80.0 in only six of his twenty seasons (see Figure 38).

The numbers he accumulated over a 20-year career are staggering – over 10,000 attempted passes, 6,300 completions, more than 500 TDs and over 70,000 yards thrown. His most impressive stat, though, is the 297 consecutive games he started.   Favre is the Carl Ripken of football.   It is just mindboggling that he did not miss a start in more than eighteen years, considering the animalistic nature of the sport of football.

In addition to his ironman streak, there is also one other record he owns that shall never be reached – his 336 career interceptions. For someone to break this record, he would have to play for 20 years tossing 17 picks per season. If they only played 15 years, they would have to throw more than 22 picks per season. When you take into account the deflation of interceptions over time, it is *extremely* unlikely that anyone will ever catch him.

NOTE: Rightly, Favre became a first-ballot HOFer in 2016.

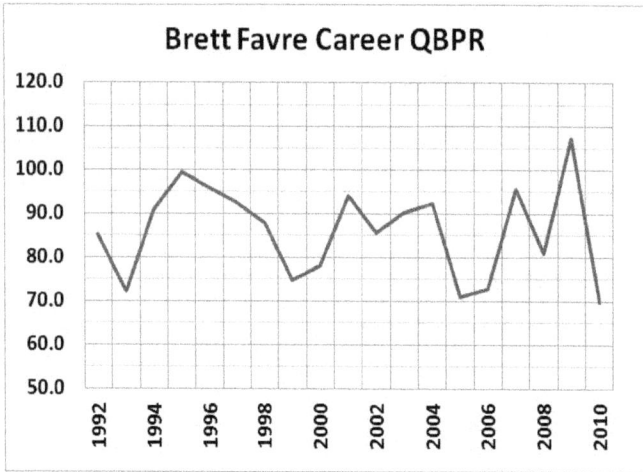

Figure 38 – Brett Favre Career QBPR

WHAT COULD HAVE BEEN

Five names are linked by the hypothetical "Can you imagine if they played a full career in the NFL?" They are Roger Staubach, Jim Kelly, Steve Young, Kurt Warner and Warren Moon.

Even with relatively shorter careers than their counterparts, the numbers that the first four accumulated impresses. Moon was the exception. Even though he played well into his 40's, he was a benchwarmer in his last few years, so they did not add significant value to his overall stats.

ROGER STAUBACH

Staubach placed fourth on the Best Ever list. Imagine just how much better he would have fared had he played longer! Staubach served four years in the Navy before finally joining the NFL at the ripe old age of 27. He played for 11 seasons but did not start in Dallas until his third year, carrying a clipboard behind starter Craig Morton. He led the Cowboys to four SBs in the 70s, winning two. In the losses, the Cowboys played two great games against the Steel Curtain, coming up short both times. In the second of those games, Staubach delivered a touchdown pass to tight end, Jimmy Smith, late in the fourth quarter that would have put the Cowboys ahead and potentially sealed the victory. Unfortunately, the ball hit Jimmy right in the chest and bounced harmlessly to the turf. Surely, Staubach still daydreams of what could have been.

In just nine years as the starting quarterback in Dallas, Staubach earned the third best regular season record ever – his team won an astounding 72% of the games he started. Only four QBs have enjoyed careers with a 70% winning record in the regular season: Peyton, Staubach, Brady and Lamonica. That is some very elite company attesting not only to their value but also to the consistency of the teams they led.

Staubach retired in 1979, and even though he missed the coming pass-inflation from the 1978 rule changes, his stats hold their own against the list as is. When we applied the inflation adjustment, his QBPR jumped from 20th to sixth overall. A terrific runner, he earned the moniker "Roger the Dodger," while still at the Navy Academy, from his mad scrambling skills. He rates as one of only nine QBs to have positive rushing yardage when we included sack yards.

When you consider the best teams and QBs of the seventies, two names rise to the top: Staubach's Cowboys and Bradshaw's Steelers. Both of them led their teams to the SB four times. Had Jackie Smith held on to that ball on their second SB meeting, Roger and Terry would have tied with identical 3-1 SB record. Instead, Bradshaw holds the best record at 4-0 while Staubach settled for a 2-2. It is scary to think how many SBs the Steelers might have won had they swapped places; Staubach would probably stand alone at the top of the Best Ever list by a large margin.

JIM KELLY

Kelly played two years in the short-lived USFL, 1984-85, where he led the league with pinball-type numbers for the Houston Gamblers and their "Run-and-Shoot" offense. When the USFL folded in 1986, Kelly joined the Buffalo Bills (they had originally drafted him in 1983), where he played for 11 years and led them to four straight SBs in the early nineties. Had Norwood not pushed that 47-yarder wide right against the Giants in the first of the four SB, who knows if the boost in confidence allows them to win at least one more? Although, realistically, the Cowboys teams they played in 1992 and 1993 were very talented, and probably the better team won both times they met.

Even though repeated knee injuries hampered his career, Kelly's grittiness was legendary and in 1990, he came back just two weeks after arthroscopic knee surgery to lead his Bills to a playoff win en route to the first of his four SBs.

Of the class of '83, widely regarded as the best QB draft ever, six were first-round draft picks. They were, in order: John Elway, Todd Blackledge, Jim Kelly, Tony Eason, Ken O'Brian and Dan Marino. Elway, Kelly and Marino all went on to Canton and rated very highly on the best of all-time list. While Marino was the better pocket passer and Elway had more SB wins, Kelly had the best combination. His aggregate passing ability, a knack for winning, and toughness sandwiched him between Marino and Elway on the Best Ever list.

Had Kelly not missed those first two seasons playing in the USFL, his career stats probably would have pushed him into the Top 10 in passing yards, TDs and few rungs higher on Best of All-Time.

STEVE YOUNG

Like Kelly, Young also played two years in the USFL, then another two very uneventful seasons for the Tampa Bay Bucs.

Traded to San Fran in 1987, he carried a clipboard for four seasons as Montana's backup. He took over the starting job for good in 1991, when Joe missed the entire year with an elbow injury he suffered against the Giants in the Conference Championship game the previous year. Young proceeded to reel off an 8-season stretch that rivals the most efficient quarterback play ever. During that time span, he completed 67% of his passes and threw 198 TDs against only 80 interceptions. In his last full year, at 37 years old, he recorded a QB passer rating of 101.1. This was a rare feat not only for the high score but also, for the advanced age at which he recorded it. Only 12 QBs have achieved a 100.0 rating after the age of 35 and Young accounts for two of those scores. Unfortunately, a series of recurring concussions ended up cutting his career short the following season, and he retired in 1999.

To supplement his high-efficiency passing game, Young also ran and scrambled superbly. His rumblin' bumblin' stumblin' 49-yard TD run in 1988 against the Minnesota Vikings routinely makes the ESPN Top 10 Best Ever highlights.

Unfortunately, for Steve, he became a victim of circumstance, missing eight years of his prime playing with the LA Galaxy of the USFL, Tampa Bay Bucs and then backing up Montana. Unfortunately, since only starts count for the postseason win metric, the years he rode the bench in San Fran do not count towards playoff appearances, which account for one-third of the win metric. Consequently, he missed the opportunity to start on two SB winning teams that would have catapulted him into the top five. Had he played his entire career in San Francisco, Young would have rewritten the record books.

KURT WARNER

Cut by the Green Bay Packers in 1994 as an undrafted free-agent, a down-and-out Warner took a job packing groceries at a local Hy-Vee in Cedar Rapids, Iowa. After some soul searching and a spiritual awakening, he decided to give pro-football one last chance. He scratched and crawled his way through the Arena Football League and the developmental European Football league for four long years before landing a roster spot in Dick Vermeil's revamped St. Louis Rams in 1998. When Trent Green went down unexpectedly with an injury during the 1999 preseason, Kurt stepped in and delivered, at the time, the second best statistical season in the history of the NFL, leading the Rams to a SB trophy and winning MVP honors along the way. He still stands as the only QB to win the SB the same season that he led the league in passing.

Two years later, his highly favored Rams lost the SB to a little-known rookie nicknamed Tom Terrific. Ironically, like Warner, Brady had taken over the QB position earlier in the year when the Patriots starting QB, Drew Bledsoe, had gone down with an injury.

After Mike Martz had driven the Rams team into the ground, Warner's last two years in St Louis were a disaster. However, after an unceremonious stop with the Giants, he revived his career in Arizona, eventually leading them to the SB in 2008. He came within a hair of winning a second SB, only to lose to Pittsburgh's Big Ben and a fantastic game-winning drive with less than a minute left. Warner's three SB appearances tie him for seventh all-time.

Over the years, Kurt developed a reputation for turning the ball over on fumbles. Against the field, he ranked in the middle of the pack in interceptions-per-attempt. However, he ranked 189th on the list fumbling the ball almost once per game. Towards the end of his career he started wearing gloves, even on the throwing hand, to help him grip the football and eliminate the bad case of fumbleitis he had developed earlier.

Warner's passing accuracy became legendary. When he retired in 2009, his completion percentage rated as the highest amongst retired QBs. In a relatively short 11-year career, Warner accumulated some very impressive stats, using the standard measure of QBPR, and joining some very elite company:

- Highest completion percentage (65.5%) ahead of Young, Montana and Favre
- Highest passing yards per game (260.8) ahead of Marino, Favre and Fouts
- Second highest career QB passer rating behind Young and ahead of Montana, Marino and Favre
- Second highest yards-per-attempt (7.95) behind Young and ahead of Starr, Unitas and Fouts

When compared to his peers inducted into the Hall of Fame, Warner exceeds most of them in QB efficiency and SB appearances. He should make the HOF – not on the first ballot, but, certainly, he belongs.

NOTE: Warner made the finalist round in 2015 and should gain induction into the HOF in 2016.

WARREN MOON

Moon boasted the rare combination of great passing and running ability. Unfortunately, due to the color of his skin, NFL teams denied him the opportunity to play in the league out of college. Not giving up, he headed north to the CFL where he honed his passing skills. In six years, he passed for a gazillion yards (more than 21,000), posted a 94.0 QBPR, earned two Offensive Player-of-the-Year awards, one league MVP, and led the Edmonton Eskimos to a 10-1 postseason record including five consecutive Grey Cup victories along the way.

The NFL could no longer ignore him, finally granting him his debut with the Houston Oilers in 1984, where he played for ten years repeating his successful pass/run formula from the CFL. From 1988 to 1992, he racked up a flashy 89 QBPR twice leading the league in yards.

After Houston, he enjoyed some success in Minnesota, and then finished out his career as a backup in Seattle and KC, retiring in 2000 at the age of 44. He probably hung around those extra years to make up for the years he missed at the beginning of his career, almost certainly wondering how different his career would have been had the NFL drafted him out of college. The HOF deservedly inducted Moon in 2006.

* One forgettable footnote on Moon – he was on the short-end of Frank Reicht "Greatest Playoff Comeback Ever" in the first round of the 1993 playoffs, when the Buffalo Bills stormed back from a 32-point deficit to beat the Oilers in overtime, 41–38. Whereas Moon could do no wrong in the first half, he threw two costly picks, including one in OT that led to the winning field goal.

THE MOST OVERRATED

Two Hall of Famers placed so poorly on all of the passing lists that we had to recheck the raw data several times to make sure. There was no mistake – Namath and Bradshaw performed very poorly from a statistical performance standpoint. Against the full field of 198 qualifying QBs, their adjusted metrics ranked as follows:

Metric	*Namath*	*Bradshaw*
Pass completion percentage	147th	133th
TDs-per-attempt	95th	11th
Interceptions-per-attempt	156nd	165th
aQBPR	104st	83th
mQBR	33st	82th
QBWR	81th	4th
tQBR	61th	12th

Broadway Joe had the double whammy going on – he performed poorly on the passing stats and just as awful on the winning list. His greatest claims to fame were leading the league in mink coats and living up to his bold prediction of one of the biggest upsets in SB history. Had his underdog Jets failed to win the SB against the mighty Colts, it is possible that the AFL-NFL mergers would have lost steam and never come to fruition. With renewed confidence in their league after the Jets victory, the AFL Kansas City Chiefs also won the SB the following year, and the merger was on. However, outside the 1969 SB win, Joe ranked average on the win metric scoring 81st in QBWR.

Bradshaw, like Namath, also was an interception machine and rated low on all the lists except TDs-per-attempt and in

QBWR. However, because he quarterbacked the Steelers dynasty of the seventies, he rose into 12th place on the Best Ever list. It is hard to imagine how many more SBs those Steelers teams could have won with better QB play.

Namath, meanwhile, ranked 61th on the Best Ever list and ran away with the Most Overrated category. While his supporters will claim that multiple knee injuries hampered and shortened his career, his QB passer rating did not significantly change from the beginning to the end of his career. It surprises that the HOF committee found him worthy of a selection. More likely, his induction came from an effort to legitimize the merger and reward key AFL players with a place in Canton.

CANTON WORTHY

NOTE: We published this Morsel in Feb 2015 before Ken Stabler died from colon cancer in July 2015. The NFL enshrined him into the HOF, posthumously, with the Class of 2016. Brett Favre also earned the first-ballot admission into the HOF in 2016. Kurt Warner made the finalist round but did not accumulate the required 80% votes on his second year of eligibility.

We discussed at length the HOF candidacy of Favre and Warner throughout this book. However, as we compiled the categorical Top 20 lists, other QBs also placed prominently ahead of some of the established members of the Canton Club.

When we mapped the 19 HOF QBs of the Modern Era on the Best Ever list, only six placed outside the Top 25: Tarkenton, Jurgensen, Fouts, Blanda, Namath and Moon. This left 13 HOF QBs in the Top 25 plus 12 other non-HOF QBs.

Of the 12 names, six of them are sure to be inducted into the Hall when their time comes: Peyton, Brady, Brees, Warner Rodgers and Roethlisberger. Most of them have the passing acumen and winning records to demand a first ballot entrance already. Of the remaining six QBs, there is one name that deserves some further analysis: Ken Stabler, who rated 22nd on the Best Ever list.

Stabler was a proven winner, ranking 14th on the QBWR list and earning one SB ring. He had a knack for dramatic comebacks and led the league in passing in 1976, the year the Raiders won the SB over the Minnesota Vikings. That 1976 season rated fourth on the Best Season list, and his 1973 campaign also ranked in the Top 20. He has been an underrated player for an Oakland team that won its fair share of games in the seventies competing against the mighty AFC Steelers. From 1972 to 1980, he won a whopping 74% of the games he started. He is also the only member of the All-70's team that did not make the HOF. His career stats hold up well against the like of other seventies players like Griese, Tarkenton and Bradshaw. Stabler's off-the-field antics probably turned off some voters and cost him a spot in Canton. The data says otherwise, though. Lefty belongs in the Hall!

THE MANNINGS

Siblings Peyton and Eli seem to enjoy a healthy competitive relationship as can be seen in their TV commercials. It would be interesting to see how they ranked against one another statistically. There are those, mostly New Yorkers, who swear that Eli is better than his big brother Peyton because he has more rings. Just for grins and giggles, we compared their QB metrics to separate fact from fiction. To make the comparison more interesting, we added Papa Archie to the mix, but mostly to check how far the apple(s) fell from the tree.

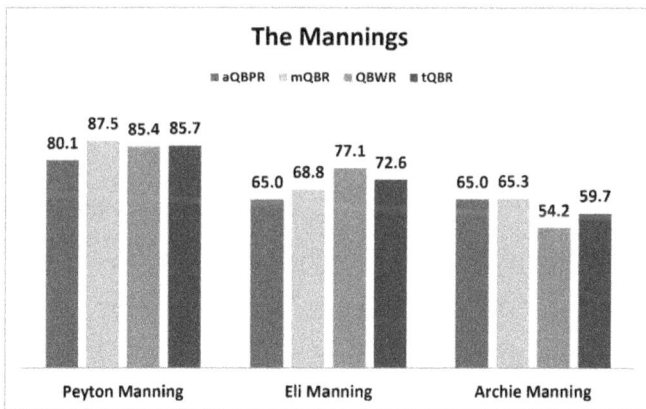

Figure 39 – Rating The Mannings

- Their QB passer rating comparison shows a marked difference between father Archie and younger brother Eli, both at 65.0, versus older sibling Peyton, a mile ahead at 80.1.
- The mQBR shows a similar trend – Archie brings up the rear at 65.3, Eli improves a bit at 68.8, and Peyton really separates himself with a Best-in-Class 87.5 score.
- For QBWR, Archie falls off a cliff at 54.2, Eli scores a decent 77.1, but Peyton again shines at 85.4.

- The final total rank, tQBR, also separates the three – Papa Manning gets dragged down to 59.7 while Eli sits with a respectable 72.7 and Peyton soars atop at 85.7.

Aside from those two SB rings, Eli's winning record does not rate as stellar. He owns a mediocre 53.0% regular season winning percentage while leading his team to the playoffs a meager 41.7% of the time. Peyton, on the other hand, rates as the third All-Time leader with a 70.2% in regular season winning percentage and first at taking his team to the postseason, an impressive 88.2% of the time. Archie, on the other hand, is the anti-Peyton. He played for the lovable loser New Orleans Saints, and his regular and postseason percentages were atrocious at 27.9% and 0.0%, respectively. He never as much as sniffed a playoff game.

Eli is an enigma. He has outstanding up years leading to Lombardi trophies, but awful down years rate usually leading the league in turnovers. However, he does sneak by his brother in one stat – normalized game-winning drives with a score of 19.6% to 19.5%. His two game-winning drives against the Golden Boy and his Patriots, in the 2007 and 2011 SBs, are a testament to the ice running through his veins when the chips are down. He is like the Namath and Bradshaw of this generation – a poor statistical quarterback who wins the big games.

So one thing in this argument is correct – Eli does have very similar stats to another Manning. It just happens to be his father, Archie. Peyton plays in another league and frankly, he should test his DNA because other than a common last name, there are no similarities between him and his brother or father.

THE BOB BEAMON AWARD

Bob Beamon stands as the case study in all Statistics classes as the classic definition of an outlier in a sports performance. Going into the 1968 Mexico City Olympics, Beamon was among the favorites to win the long jump event. His personal best stood at 27' 4" while the world record, set three years earlier, sat at 27' 4 ¾". On October 18, Beamon sprinted down the lane, jumped like never before and landed 29' 2 ½" later, destroying the previous long jump record. In a sport measured in quarters of an inch, his record-setting performance beat the standing mark by almost 2 feet! This record stood from 1968 until 1991 when Mike Powell finally bettered it by two inches, and where it has remained until today. Beamon never again broke the 27 feet barrier in competition, but his Olympic jump remains the second longest jump ever, even 50 years later.

While researching this book, we stumbled upon an obscure Beamonesque statistic. In 1960, a little-known quarterback named Milt Plum led the NFL with a QB passer rating of 110.4. Huh, Milt who? It turns out that Plum rated as an above average journeyman with a lifetime QBPR of 72.2, drafted in the second round out of Penn State and played most of his career in Cleveland and Detroit. Outside of a Pro Bowl appearances after the 1960 season, and an above average follow-up year, nothing in his resume before or after hinted at such a spectacular season. Before the phenomenal 1960 season, his scored a best QBPR rating of 87.2 while after a 90.3. While very respectable scores for that era, they fell more than 20 points short of his incredible 110.4 season. In fact, statistically, his 110.4 score rated more than two and a half standard deviations away from the mean of

72.2. The chance of this occurring was less than 1.3%! As a result, Plum's record-setting performance stood for almost 30 years until Montana broke it in 1989 with an 112.4. Milt's staggering QBPR score even rated him #1 on the Best Season Ever list.

So what explained this unexpected outlier performance? In Beamon's case, he had the high altitude of Mexico City and the maximum allowable wind helping him down that lane. In Plum's case, we suspect that the answer partially lies in the dilution of the talent pool created by the startup AFL that opened its doors that same year. NFL players defected to the new league in the early sixties, and it shows prominently in the short-lived rise in the NFL QB passer rating (dark gray line in the chart below). The established NFL QBs quickly took advantage of the depleted defenses. After the merger, the average scores came back down to their normal values in the 60's.

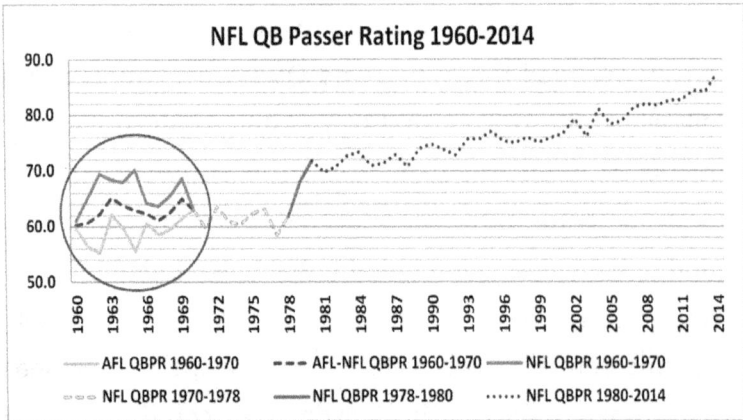

Figure 40 – NFL-AFL QB Passer Rating

As with Beamon's jump, Plum's performance was so far out there that even the expert explanations fell short. Scientists determined that the high altitude and aid of the wind would have improved Beamon's jump by almost a foot, well short of the 21 inches he gained over the previous record. With Plum, even with a hefty 10-point spike in QBPR added to his previous high of 87.2, he would still only score in the high nineties, more than 10 points short of his remarkable 110.4 QBPR.

Some things are just inexplicable, especially in sports.

FINAL WORDS

The NFL Quarterback remains one of the most glamorous positions in American sports. In this book, we evaluated the performance of more than 1,600 starting quarterbacks to have played since 1960 then rated them to identify the one percenters. As we first discovered, the NFL benchmark for rating QBs has needed revamping for a while. So, we broke down the metric into its essential components, and then rebuilt it accounting for numerous factors that leveled the playing field for several generations of great quarterbacks from the last 55 years.

Four factors contributed to the statistical inflation and obsolescence of the NFL passer metric, the QBPR. First, due to an oversight in the development of the original formula, the QB passer rating metric excluded the stats of the AFL players, so right off the bat, after the merger the metric was off by four points. Second, downfield contact rule changes along the way altered the game dramatically, allowing QBs to attempt more passes, complete them at a higher rate and toss fewer interceptions. Third, the style of play changed considerably with the introduction of the West Coast and Air Coryell offenses that took advantage of the new rules. Finally, the metric did not incorporate other aspects of the quarterbacking position like running, scrambling, avoiding sacks and fumbling. More importantly, it neglected entirely all of the aspects of winning, such as regular season wins and losses, game-winning drives and postseason success.

From Green Bay legends (Starr, Favre and Rodger) to undefeated multiple Super Bowl winners (Bradshaw, Montana,

Aikman and Plunkett), we re-rated all of the QBs going back to 1960 according to the new standards of measurement: the adjusted QB passer rating (aQBPR), the modified QB rating (mQBR), the QB win rating (QBWR) and the total QB rating (tQBR). These four new metrics incorporated all the missing factors, thereby allowing for a fair comparison of quarterbacks that played in different decades with different rules and styles of play. The aQBPR normalized the effect of statistical inflation. The mQBR incorporated the missing dimensions of the QB position. The QBWR assessed the impact of winning. Lastly, the combination of these three metrics provided the basis for the final metric, tQBR, which provides an unbiased ranking and rating of the top quarterbacks of the Modern Era.

So, what did we conclude from all these metrics, acronyms, formulas and statistical mumbo-jumbo?

We learned that the supporting cast had a huge influence in wins and losses. The win rating metric, QBWR, for several HOF caliber players pushed them out of the Top 20 All-Time QBs. Players like Fouts, Tarkenton and Jurgensen, fell into this category. We also found that the QB running dimension is overrated if not combined with an ability to avoid sacks or more importantly, to pass the rock. Quarterbacks with one-dimensional games did not rate well on the Best Ever list. QBs with great arms but poor run/sack skills, like Bernie Kosar, Jim Hart and Jeff George, did not crack the Top 40. The same rang true about great runners with limited passing skills like Daunte Cunningham, Michael Vick and Randall Cunningham.

As far as the question posed at the beginning of the book – "Who is the Best of All-Time?" The Best Pure Passer is Steve Young. The QB with the Best Combined Skills is Peyton Manning. The Winningest QB is Tom Brady.

The Best Ever title came down to two QBs. After the stat inflation was deflated, the passer rating metric corrected, the non-passing QB factors factored and winning aspects included, two men stood at the top of the mountain, their respective tQBR scores separated by the slightest of margins (0.1) but head-and-shoulders above the rest (~4.0) – Brady and Montana. These two are 1A and 1B, statistically the same, but since we have to declare a winner, in a dead heat Tom Terrific takes the top spot as the Best Ever. If your team trailed with less than two minutes and you had to pick a QB to drive to your team to a win, there is no question that either of these would be your top choice. Tom Terrific or Joe Cool – you could not go wrong with either.

The Golden Boy, Thomas Edward Patrick Brady, took over the top spot with his fourth Super Bowl win in 2014. He might even widen the gap if his Patriots continue their winning ways. His unbelievable 2007 campaign was just his way of letting Peyton know that he could also put up ridiculous video game-type numbers when necessary. Brady owns nine game-winning drives in the playoffs and three in the SB, including a 10-point fourth quarter comeback against the Seahawks in SB49 – the man is clutch. If that was not enough, just to rub it in, he also leads in another category – hottest wife. Clearly, he belongs at the top.

Montana's good looks and calm demeanor were legendary. He always saved his best performance for the biggest stage earning three Super Bowl MVP's in four appearances along with four Lombardi trophies. In the famous words of the late Stuart Scott, Joe was "as cool as the other side of the pillow."

Peyton, at number three, slipped past Staubach into third by finishing his career à la Elway – walking away from the game with one final Lombardi Trophy tucked nicely under his arm. Peyton redefined the position of Field General with his no-huddle antics and pre-snap misdirection. His preparation, practice regimen and disappointment prune-face have no equal. Omaha will live in infamy forever.

Number four on the list, Staubach, is a legend on and off the football field. He integrated passing ability, a knack for winning, unparalleled leadership and the added dimension of scrambling. Roger "The Dodger" won two Super Bowls and faced off against a strong Steelers team on two other occasions, coming up just short both times. What is unusual about Staubach is that he did not start his career until he was 27. He attended the U.S. Naval Academy where he won a Heisman Trophy, and after graduation, served his country for four years in the U.S. Navy, including a tour of duty in Vietnam. Roger remains, no doubt, exemplary on and off the field and an All-Time Great.

At fifth and seventh, Rodgers and Roethlisberger lead a promising group of active quarterbacks that will take the baton from Brady and Peyton. Rodgers took over the top spot from Young as the best pure passer ever in 2014 and then gave it back with a sub par 2015 campaign. However, if he can lead his team to another championship or two, he could potentially leapfrog a couple of spots on the All-Time rank. Roethlisberger, on the other hand, is a beast. He balances heavy-duty stats with a winning attitude. His last minute drive to beat the Arizona Cardinals in the 2008 Super Bowl cemented his clutch reputation. It was appropriate that these two squared off in the 2010 SB with Rodgers coming out on top.

The players from sixties also fared strongly in the Top 20 list: Bart Starr took sixth place, Johnny Unitas ninth, Daryle Lamonica tenth and Len Dawson 14th. They ranked as the best from a decade of formidable quarterbacks that also included Sonny Jurgensen. Unfortunately for Jurgensen, like in the case of Fouts, he played with a weak supporting cast that held him back, and he never played as a starter in the postseason.

Steve Young filled the last spot in the Top 10 coming in eighth place. His passing acumen and winning attitude took a back seat to #2 on the list, Montana, for what must have felt like an eternity in San Fran.

The great QB Class of 1983 placed three outstanding players in the top 20. Marino (11th), Kelly (13th) and Elway (18th) took their rightful place in Canton, all entering on the first ballot. Of this trio, Marino was the best passer, Kelly the grittiest and Elway the winningest.

Bradshaw and Aikman filled the 12th and 16th spots in the Top 20. Each of them led dynasties to the Promised Land never losing in the big game. Montana with four, Eli and Plunkett with two are the other QBs with multiple appearances never to lose the championship.

Lastly, Drew Brees (#15), Kurt Warner (#17), Brett Favre (#19) and unexpectedly Joe Flacco (#20) round out the Top 20. Brees still has some gas left in the tank and he might reach some rarified air on the career totals list, perhaps even eclipsing Favre and Manning in passing yards. A finalist in 2015, Warner should make the Hall soon, which will open the door to the "Greatest Show on Turf" receivers, Isaac Bruce and Torry Holt. As expected, Favre earned entrance into Canton on his first ballot in 2016. Flacco on the other hand, surprised with this placement as his passing metrics rated average. However, like Bradshaw and Eli, he has shined in the postseason and owns a terrific winning metric that carried him.

The Top 20 is chock-full of the best NFL quarterbacks of their generation. Each passed the torch to the next. Starr and Unitas gave it to Staubach and Bradshaw who in turn delivered it to Montana and Marino. Aikman and Young took it from there, handing it off to Peyton and Brady, who will pass the torch to Rodgers and Roethlisberger. Each generation had their best, and these All-Time greats fit the bill for the last five and half decades.

We also had plenty of surprising results along the way. Who 'da thunk that Roethlisberger would rank so highly on so many Top 20 lists? Or that Griese would place ahead of Marino on normalized TDs-per-attempt? Or that little known Milt Plum would own the Best Season Ever?

Even more surprising were the underperformers. Hall of Famers Joe Namath and Terry Bradshaw rated poorly on all of the QB performance metrics except for one – Super Bowl wins when they counted. In time, Eli Manning and Joe Flacco will join them on this list – all they do is win Super Bowls, in spite of some mediocre regular seasons.

The future of the quarterback position looks bright as a crop of very talented QBs looks just as exciting, gritty and able as their peers from yesteryear. Joe Flacco and Matt Ryan alongside newbies Russell Wilson, Andrew Luck, Kirk Cousins and Derek Carr will carry on the excitement and glamor of the position for years to come. In just three years, Wilson is quickly distancing himself from the rest of the field in a way that is reminiscent of number one on the list – Brady. Their showdown in SB 49 showed that Wilson not quite ready and the old man not quite willing to pass the torch just yet.

We have one last disclaimer – this book focused solely on isolating and normalizing the statistical performance of the QB position in order to judge the best from the last half century. However, we purposely avoided a closely related subject that we will tackle in the next book of this series "Football Morsels: The Supporting Cast." As covered throughout, football is a team sport and, while the QB position has a huge impact on the outcome, the QB cannot protect the pocket, tote the rock, catch the ball, kick field goals, play defense or coach the team.

The Litmus Test for the supporting cast argument is to play "what if" scenarios. What if Staubach and Bradshaw switch teams – how many more Super Bowls do the Steelers win? What if the Patriots drafted Peyton and he gets mentored by The Hoodie and his winning ways – does Brady have as much success elsewhere? Do the Patriots win multiple Super Bowls with Peyton at the helm? To add even more to the QB discussion, we will break down these questions, along with a thorough analysis of the running attack, receiving corps, defensive units and coaching aspects of the supporting cast in the next installment of the Football Morsels series.

So there it is! The top quarterbacks of the modern era – impartially chosen, statistically analyzed and clearly defined. The collective facts presented eliminated the bias and emotion that always clutter the "Best of All Time" discussions. That said, even though we impartially ranked and rated the top QBs of all-time and regardless of the regression analysis, the statistical significance and the ironclad conclusions, *Marino will always be number one on my list.*

APPENDICES

APPENDIX A

References used in this book to mine raw data for QB passing, running and receiving stats included:

www.nfl-reference.com

www.espn.go.com/nfl/statistics

 www.nfl.com/stats/player

www.profootballHOF.com

www.wikipedia.com

We used the Bureau of Labor Statistics CPI inflation calculator for the gas price reference:

www.bls.gov/data/inflation_calculator.htm

APPENDIX B

List of qualifying QBs (198) with a minimum of 8 years in the league, 5 as starter, 600 pass attempts and 5,000 pass yards:

No	Name	No	Name	No	Name	No	Name
1	Aaron Brooks	51	David Woodley	101	John Brodie	151	Rich Gannon
2	Aaron Rodgers	52	Derek Anderson	102	John Elway	152	Richard Todd
3	Alex Smith	53	Don Majkowski	103	John Friesz	153	Rick Mirer
4	Andy Dalton	54	Don Meredith	104	John Hadl	154	Rodney Peete
5	Archie Manning	55	Donovan McNabb	105	Johnny Unitas	155	Roger Staubach
6	Babe Parilli	56	Doug Flutie	106	Jon Kitna	156	Roman Gabriel
7	Bart Starr	57	Doug Williams	107	Josh Freeman	157	Ron Jaworski
8	Ben Roethlisberger	58	Drew Bledsoe	108	Josh McCown	158	Rudy Bukich
9	Bernie Kosar	59	Drew Brees	109	Ken Anderson	159	Ryan Fitzpatrick
10	Bert Jones	60	Earl Morrall	110	Ken O'Brien	160	Sam Bradford
11	Bill Kenney	61	Eli Manning	111	Ken Stabler	161	Scott Hunter
12	Bill Munson	62	Elvis Grbac	112	Kent Graham	162	Scott Mitchell
13	Bill Nelsen	63	Eric Hipple	113	Kerry Collins	163	Shaun Hill
14	Billy Joe Tolliver	64	Erik Kramer	114	King Hill	164	Sonny Jurgensen
15	Billy Kilmer	65	Fran Tarkenton	115	Kordell Stewart	165	Stan Humphries
16	Billy Wade	66	Frank Ryan	116	Kurt Warner	166	Steve Bartkowski
17	Bob Avellini	67	Gary Cuozzo	117	Kyle Boller	167	Steve Beuerlein
18	Bob Berry	68	Gary Danielson	118	Kyle Orton	168	Steve Bono
19	Bob Griese	69	Gary Hogeboom	119	Len Dawson	169	Steve DeBerg
20	Bob Lee	70	George Blanda	120	Lynn Dickey	170	Steve Fuller
21	Bobby Douglass	71	Greg Landry	121	Marc Bulger	171	Steve Grogan
22	Bobby Hebert	72	Gus Frerotte	122	Marc Wilson	172	Steve McNair
23	Boomer Esiason	73	Jack Concannon	123	Mark Brunell	173	Steve Ramsey
24	Brad Johnson	74	Jack Kemp	124	Mark Malone	174	Steve Spurrier
25	Brett Favre	75	Jack Trudeau	125	Mark Rypien	175	Steve Tensi
26	Brian Griese	76	Jake Delhomme	126	Mark Sanchez	176	Steve Young
27	Brian Sipe	77	Jake Plummer	127	Marty Domres	177	Tarvaris Jackson
28	Bubby Brister	78	James Harris	128	Matt Cassel	178	Terry Bradshaw
29	Byron Leftwich	79	Jason Campbell	129	Matt Hasselbeck	179	Tim Couch
30	Cam Newton	80	Jay Cutler	130	Matt Ryan	180	Tobin Rote
31	Carson Palmer	81	Jay Fiedler	131	Matt Schaub	181	Tom Brady
32	Chad Henne	82	Jay Schroeder	132	Matthew Stafford	182	Tom Flores
33	Chad Pennington	83	Jeff Blake	133	Michael Vick	183	Tommy Kramer
34	Charley Johnson	84	Jeff Garcia	134	Mike Livingston	184	Tommy Maddox
35	Charlie Batch	85	Jeff George	135	Mike Pagel	185	Tony Banks
36	Chris Chandler	86	Jeff Hostetler	136	Mike Phipps	186	Tony Eason
37	Chris Miller	87	Jim Everett	137	Mike Taliaferro	187	Tony Romo
38	Cotton Davidson	88	Jim Harbaugh	138	Mike Tomczak	188	Trent Dilfer
39	Craig Morton	89	Jim Hart	139	Milt Plum	189	Trent Green
40	Dan Fouts	90	Jim Kelly	140	Neil Lomax	190	Troy Aikman
41	Dan Marino	91	Jim McMahon	141	Neil O'Donnell	191	Vince Evans
42	Dan Pastorini	92	Jim Ninowski	142	Norm Snead	192	Vince Ferragamo
43	Danny White	93	Jim Plunkett	143	Pat Haden	193	Vince Young
44	Daryle Lamonica	94	Jim Zorn	144	Peyton Manning	194	Vinny Testaverde
45	Daunte Culpepper	95	Joe Ferguson	145	Phil Simms	195	Virgil Carter
46	Dave Brown	96	Joe Flacco	146	Philip Rivers	196	Wade Wilson
47	Dave Krieg	97	Joe Montana	147	Randall Cunningham	197	Warren Moon
48	Dave Wilson	98	Joe Namath	148	Randy Johnson	198	Zeke Bratkowski
49	David Carr	99	Joe Theismann	149	Randy Wright		
50	David Garrard	100	Joey Harrington	150	Rex Grossman		

APPENDIX C

Statistics of the Top 50 quarterbacks:

No	Name	Games Started	Pass Cmp	Pass Att	Cmp %	Pass Yds	Pass Yds/Att	Pass TDs	Pass Int	Sacks	Sack Yds	GWD	Win %
1	Tom Brady	223	4,953	7,792	63.6%	58,028	7.45	428	150	402	2,509	48	77.1%
2	Joe Montana	164	3,409	5,391	63.2%	40,551	7.52	273	139	313	2,095	33	71.3%
3	Peyton Manning	265	6,125	9,380	65.3%	71,940	7.67	539	251	303	1,953	55	70.2%
4	Roger Staubach	114	1,685	2,958	57.0%	22,700	7.67	153	109	313	2,154	23	74.6%
5	Aaron Rodgers	119	2,633	4,047	65.1%	32,399	8.01	257	65	306	1,917	14	67.2%
6	Bart Starr	157	1,808	3,149	57.4%	24,718	7.85	152	138	338	2,866	18	61.8%
7	Ben Roethlisberger	169	3,476	5,423	64.1%	42,995	7.93	272	147	439	2,867	36	66.9%
8	Steve Young	143	2,667	4,149	64.3%	33,124	7.98	232	107	358	2,055	17	65.7%
9	Johnny Unitas	185	2,830	5,186	54.6%	40,239	7.76	290	253	401	3,113	29	64.5%
10	Daryle Lamonica	88	1,288	2,601	49.5%	19,154	7.36	164	138	159	1,378	17	78.4%
11	Dan Marino	240	4,967	8,358	59.4%	61,361	7.34	420	252	270	1,930	51	61.3%
12	Terry Bradshaw	158	2,025	3,901	51.9%	27,989	7.17	212	210	307	2,694	27	67.7%
13	Jim Kelly	160	2,874	4,779	60.1%	35,467	7.42	237	175	323	2,427	29	63.1%
14	Len Dawson	159	2,136	3,741	57.1%	28,711	7.67	239	183	378	3,407	18	61.6%
15	Drew Brees	216	5,365	8,085	66.4%	60,903	7.53	428	205	331	2,363	38	57.4%
16	Troy Aikman	165	2,898	4,715	61.5%	32,942	6.99	165	141	259	1,748	21	57.0%
17	Kurt Warner	116	2,666	4,070	65.5%	32,344	7.95	208	128	260	1,669	14	57.8%
18	John Elway	231	4,123	7,250	56.9%	51,475	7.10	300	226	516	3,785	46	64.3%
19	Brett Favre	298	6,300	10,169	62.0%	71,838	7.06	508	336	525	3,487	45	62.4%
20	Joe Flacco	122	2,479	4,070	60.9%	28,322	6.96	162	102	257	1,833	24	61.5%
21	Bob Griese	151	1,926	3,429	56.2%	25,092	7.32	192	172	339	2,967	20	61.9%
22	Ken Stabler	146	2,270	3,793	59.8%	27,938	7.37	194	222	281	2,514	26	66.1%
23	Tony Romo	127	2,826	4,331	65.3%	34,154	7.89	247	117	248	1,672	30	61.4%
24	Joe Theismann	124	2,044	3,602	56.7%	25,206	7.00	160	138	340	2,757	24	62.1%
25	Danny White	94	1,744	2,922	59.7%	21,711	7.43	153	129	238	2,053	16	67.4%
26	Mark Rypien	78	1,466	2,613	56.1%	18,473	7.07	115	88	97	664	12	60.3%
27	Fran Tarkenton	239	3,686	6,467	57.0%	47,003	7.27	342	266	600	5,265	34	53.1%
28	Jack Kemp	100	1,372	2,934	46.8%	20,290	6.92	109	177	215	1,963	11	63.5%
29	Philip Rivers	160	3,462	5,339	64.8%	41,447	7.76	281	135	325	1,980	25	57.5%
30	Frank Ryan	87	1,090	2,133	51.1%	16,042	7.52	149	111	200	1,662	9	67.2%
31	Jim McMahon	97	1,492	2,573	58.0%	18,148	7.05	100	90	226	1,344	14	69.1%
32	Earl Morrall	100	1,354	2,611	51.9%	20,346	7.79	156	139	263	2,152	13	64.5%
33	Sonny Jurgensen	147	2,433	4,262	57.1%	32,224	7.56	255	189	317	2,607	14	48.7%
34	Matt Ryan	126	2,915	4,530	64.3%	32,757	7.23	202	107	218	1,443	31	58.7%
35	Donovan McNabb	161	3,170	5,374	59.0%	37,276	6.94	234	117	410	2,626	25	61.2%
36	Eli Manning	183	3,695	6,227	59.3%	44,191	7.10	294	199	307	2,137	33	53.0%
37	Brad Johnson	125	2,668	4,326	61.7%	29,054	6.72	166	122	251	1,616	27	57.6%
38	Ken Anderson	172	2,654	4,475	59.3%	32,838	7.34	197	160	398	2,875	15	52.9%
39	Andy Dalton	77	1,556	2,497	62.3%	18,008	7.21	124	73	140	813	16	65.6%
40	Dan Fouts	171	3,297	5,604	58.8%	43,040	7.68	254	242	319	2,304	26	50.6%
41	Chad Pennington	81	1,632	2,471	66.0%	17,823	7.21	102	64	162	965	11	54.3%
42	Bernie Kosar	101	1,879	3,164	59.4%	22,084	6.98	116	84	250	1,528	17	50.0%
43	Tony Eason	46	832	1,423	58.5%	10,126	7.12	57	45	160	1,230	7	58.7%
44	George Blanda	106	1,911	4,007	47.7%	26,920	6.72	236	277	142	1,271	11	51.4%
45	Craig Morton	137	1,929	3,547	54.4%	26,386	7.44	174	174	389	2,912	22	58.8%
46	Jeff Hostetler	83	1,357	2,338	58.0%	16,430	7.03	94	71	207	1,158	12	61.4%
47	Doug Williams	81	1,240	2,507	49.5%	16,998	6.78	100	93	84	734	21	47.5%
48	Jeff Garcia	116	2,264	3,676	61.6%	25,537	6.95	161	83	181	947	19	50.0%
49	Jake Delhomme	96	1,741	2,932	59.4%	20,975	7.15	126	101	168	1,267	25	58.3%
50	Stan Humphries	81	1,431	2,516	56.9%	17,191	6.83	89	84	144	1,182	12	61.7%

APPENDIX D

QB metrics of the Top 50 quarterbacks:

No	Name	QBPR	aQBPR	z-aQBPR	mQBR	z-mQBPR	QBWR	z-QBWR	tQBR	z-tQBR
1	Tom Brady	96.37	78.76	1.51	81.39	1.84	97.77	3.89	89.32	2.83
2	Joe Montana	92.26	83.96	2.16	87.31	2.58	91.79	3.14	89.22	2.82
3	Peyton Manning	96.46	80.07	1.68	87.54	2.61	85.36	2.34	85.70	2.38
4	Roger Staubach	83.42	82.35	1.96	79.54	1.61	91.02	3.04	85.56	2.36
5	Aaron Rodgers	104.13	84.68	2.25	82.76	2.01	82.00	1.92	82.57	1.99
6	Bart Starr	80.47	80.43	1.72	78.02	1.42	86.44	2.47	82.47	1.98
7	Ben Roethlisberger	93.96	75.32	1.08	74.93	1.03	85.78	2.39	80.39	1.72
8	Steve Young	96.81	86.49	2.48	83.58	2.11	75.19	1.07	79.68	1.63
9	Johnny Unitas	78.20	78.24	1.45	78.69	1.50	80.72	1.76	79.66	1.62
10	Daryle Lamonica	72.94	73.41	0.84	79.35	1.59	80.54	1.73	79.35	1.59
11	Dan Marino	86.38	76.89	1.28	83.24	2.07	75.56	1.11	78.76	1.51
12	Terry Bradshaw	70.92	68.42	0.22	68.97	0.29	87.84	2.65	78.35	1.46
13	Jim Kelly	84.39	74.97	1.04	76.38	1.21	80.05	1.67	78.07	1.43
14	Len Dawson	82.56	82.89	2.03	78.82	1.52	76.30	1.20	77.97	1.41
15	Drew Brees	95.85	77.86	1.40	83.17	2.06	73.62	0.87	77.87	1.40
16	Troy Aikman	81.62	71.00	0.54	75.06	1.05	81.03	1.80	77.64	1.37
17	Kurt Warner	93.71	78.57	1.49	76.70	1.25	77.23	1.32	77.16	1.31
18	John Elway	79.86	70.44	0.47	70.59	0.49	83.37	2.09	76.97	1.29
19	Brett Favre	86.03	72.58	0.74	75.35	1.09	77.20	1.32	76.00	1.17
20	Joe Flacco	84.66	65.06	-0.20	66.72	0.01	85.46	2.35	75.92	1.16
21	Bob Griese	77.14	76.31	1.21	75.73	1.13	75.75	1.14	75.80	1.14
22	Ken Stabler	75.31	71.91	0.65	73.80	0.89	77.68	1.38	75.55	1.11
23	Tony Romo	97.07	78.25	1.45	79.93	1.66	71.31	0.58	75.45	1.10
24	Joe Theismann	77.37	71.61	0.62	73.18	0.81	77.68	1.38	75.27	1.08
25	Danny White	81.84	74.33	0.96	72.79	0.77	76.57	1.24	74.84	1.02
26	Mark Rypien	78.93	69.45	0.35	74.39	0.96	76.09	1.18	74.74	1.01
27	Fran Tarkenton	80.35	80.11	1.68	80.81	1.77	68.61	0.24	74.64	1.00
28	Jack Kemp	57.11	57.18	-1.19	59.66	-0.88	90.08	2.93	74.63	0.99
29	Philip Rivers	95.47	76.41	1.22	77.48	1.35	71.25	0.57	74.25	0.95
30	Frank Ryan	77.61	77.93	1.41	74.50	0.98	72.98	0.79	74.08	0.93
31	Jim McMahon	78.17	69.66	0.37	71.84	0.65	75.83	1.15	73.62	0.87
32	Earl Morrall	75.50	75.58	1.11	72.81	0.77	73.42	0.84	73.39	0.84
33	Sonny Jurgensen	82.62	82.69	2.00	86.89	2.53	60.72	-0.74	73.39	0.84
34	Matt Ryan	90.86	71.14	0.56	75.73	1.13	71.87	0.65	73.34	0.83
35	Donovan McNabb	85.58	70.07	0.43	70.02	0.42	75.40	1.09	72.71	0.76
36	Eli Manning	83.52	64.96	-0.21	68.80	0.27	77.08	1.30	72.56	0.74
37	Brad Johnson	82.50	69.05	0.30	72.02	0.67	73.38	0.84	72.40	0.72
38	Ken Anderson	81.86	78.51	1.48	80.57	1.74	64.63	-0.25	72.40	0.72
39	Andy Dalton	88.43	67.97	0.16	71.61	0.62	72.77	0.76	71.83	0.64
40	Dan Fouts	80.23	74.71	1.01	77.58	1.36	66.47	-0.02	71.74	0.63
41	Chad Pennington	90.14	74.47	0.98	75.49	1.10	67.88	0.15	71.58	0.61
42	Bernie Kosar	81.81	73.06	0.80	75.07	1.05	68.46	0.22	71.57	0.61
43	Tony Eason	80.63	72.72	0.76	70.60	0.49	72.03	0.67	71.52	0.61
44	George Blanda	60.65	59.06	-0.95	68.25	0.20	76.62	1.24	71.52	0.61
45	Craig Morton	74.31	72.33	0.71	71.70	0.63	70.95	0.53	71.39	0.59
46	Jeff Hostetler	80.48	70.25	0.45	68.71	0.26	73.55	0.86	71.28	0.58
47	Doug Williams	69.39	62.61	-0.51	68.68	0.25	74.95	1.03	71.20	0.57
48	Jeff Garcia	87.54	73.17	0.81	75.28	1.08	67.19	0.07	71.03	0.54
49	Jake Delhomme	81.35	65.40	-0.16	66.29	-0.05	75.64	1.12	70.88	0.53
50	Stan Humphries	75.83	65.47	-0.15	68.73	0.26	73.36	0.84	70.72	0.51

GLOSSARY

QBPR (Quarterback passer rating): metric for rating quarterback passer developed by the NFL and instituted in 1973 which takes into account passing stats including attempts, completed, yards, TDs and interceptions

aQBPR (adjusted QBPR): Proprietary inflation-adjustment to the NFL QBPR metric based on the inflation regression analysis described in this book for NFL quarterbacks since 1960

mQBR (modified QB rating): Proprietary metric defined in this book that includes modifications to the QBPR and incorporates other dimensions of the quarterbacking position including rushing, sacks, receiving and fumbling.

QBWR (Quarterback win rating): Proprietary metric defined in this book to rate winning. The metric assigns a weighted value based on regular season, game-winning drives and postseason record.

tQBR (total QB rating): Proprietary formula defined in this book to rank the Best Ever at the QB position. It combines the inflation-adjusted mQBR and the win metric QBWR.

BIOGRAPHY

Julio C Castañeda Jr emigrated from Cuba to the US in 1974, grew up in South Florida and currently resides in San Jose, California, with his wife and youngest son. He graduated from Georgia Tech with a Master of Science in Mechanical Engineering and has worked for Motorola and Google for more than 25 years in product development, R&D and manufacturing. Over the course of his career, Julio has earned a Master Six Sigma Black Belt, been granted 48 US patents and authored numerous technical reports on a broad range of engineering topics. He has always been an avid sports fan fascinated by the statistical aspect of the game. In this book, Julio uses his technical acumen and expertise in analyzing data, to tackle the normalizing of performance and QB stats over the last 50 years. He developed four new metrics to account for stat inflation, missing dimensions of the QB position and winning record to rank and rate the best QB of the modern era of football. His statistical approach and data based conclusions provide a balanced and unbiased approach to accurately weigh the different aspects of the quarterbacking position and determine the Best Ever.